Jim - thought eg

Best wishes -

Bea Cornelius

7-95

W9-ARW-322

The Redemption Of Corporal Nolan Giles

Jeane Heimberger Candido

Jeane Heimberger Candido

THE REDEMPTION OF CORPORAL NOLAN GILES
Copyright © 1994 by
Jeane Heimberger Candido
Published by
PRIDE PUBLICATIONS

Cover artwork by Barbara Eisenhardt.

All rights reserved, including the right to reproduce this book
or portions thereof in any form whatsoever. Address inquires
for reviews to Pride Publications.

ISBN 1-886383-14-6

Library Of Congress Registered.

First printing May, 1995.
9 8 7 6 5 4 3 2

Printed in the United States Of America by Morris Printing.

Acknowledgements

During the course of researching and writing this book, I have made many important discoveries: coffee can be reheated in a microwave only five times before it glows in the dark; breathmints make a poor substitute for supper; and an electron microscope is a helpful tool in reading the fine print of research documents. I have also discovered that I have been blessed with family, friends, and supporters in abundance. Artists, librarians, re-enactors, historians, curators, and magazine editors have taken time out of their very demanding schedules to encourage and assist me. I have found "History People" to be among the most magnanimous in the world. Without their guidance and aid I could not have enjoyed the experience of writing this book.

The staffs of the Ohio Historical Society and the Delaware County Historical Society have been most cooperative in making available the newspapers, letters, atlases, and documents that were essential in reconstructing the nineteenth-century Ohio in which my characters lived. The guides and staff members of the National Park Service, who maintain the Civil War battlefields as living history, work enthusiastically to bring the drama and color of those long-ago events to life. They have made my every visit as much a first-person encounter with the past as possible.

My publisher Jennifer DiMarco and her mothers have made the process of a first book as painless as possible. This benevolence extended to words of consolation and encouragement through the black holes of deadline and white paper anxiety. My friends and co-workers at Barnes & Noble Bookstores were patient and understanding of a poor soul who commutes to the twentieth century only to work. David Dean and the staff of Kinko Printing somehow always got the copies no matter how bad my deadline and their backlog.

I was most blessed to have the support of Barbara Eisenhardt, an artist and painter of enormous talent and reputation to research and design the cover. Historian Larry Cosner and Roger Long, associate editor of *Gettysburg Magazine,* were most generous in rushing research inspite of busy schedules of their own.

I am deeply indebted for the support of David, Robin and Jason Roth, Michael Bergman, and Gary Milligan of *Blue & Gray Magazine.* David, founder and editor, extended the use of his magnificent library and resource facilities for this project as often as I asked. Without their support this book could not have been possible.

James Baugess, educator, historian, and friend, was kind enough to fight his way through the no-man's land of preliminary drafts to offer advice and suggestions on improving the finished product. Howard Popowski is a repository of more Civil War facts, footnotes, orders of battle and minutia than the Library of Congress. Not only did he go above and beyond the call of duty allowing precious volumes of reference to melt out of his bookshelves onto mine, but he instructed me in the School of the Soldier and taught me the intricacies of loading and shooting an 1861-vintage Enfield. When he isn't torturing his sainted wife and the cats rehearsing for another performance of the Camp Chase Fifes and Drums, Howard writes a pretty mean novel in his own "write".

I cannot say enough about the love and support of my parents Clara and Richard Foutz. My children Anne Marie and Robert Vincent, loved and encouraged me more than I can ever adequately describe here. They are both in "History Recovery" finding relief now from the emotional battering of all those endless battle-field treks, conventions, mini and maxi television series and discussion groups they have been forced to endure. How can I ever thank my husband Richard Francis Candido, First Lieutenant, Corps of Engineers, Vietnam, retired? In the nearly twenty-one years of marriage he has risked snake bite, fire ants, sunstroke, and beriberi traveling the length and breadth of almost every battlefield maintained by the National Park Service and a few that aren't. Throughout the writing and rewriting of this book he has kept his equilibrium and sense of humor.

—JHC
January, 1995

Foreward

In studying and writing about the Civil War, I do not seek to glorify war, but to try to understand it; to gain insight into its causes and to appreciate the truth that some people are burnished while others are burnt by the experience. War is the hard combustion of ideals and dreams that forms diamonds — heroes and heroines, incidents of valor and inspiration, and finally a greater appreciation for the price of peace. A price of war was paid in the 620,000 lives of young men, the tears and dreams of men and women, and the fortunes of a nation.

The causes of the Civil War are not yet resolved. Some argue that it was fought to preserve the Union, others maintain it was waged to free the slaves. The historian embraces both. But why did the soldier fight? Was he motivated to enlist for causes so noble as freedom or union or was he seeking a respite from the farms and factories that regulated his life? But the war was no caper, it raged longer and cost more than any prophet could have projected. If battle or sickness did not kill him, the ninety-day summer soldier matured into the three-year veteran who weathered the long winters of fighting. When their enlistments expired but there was more war to be fought, an astonishing number re-enlisted and went back to the line to see it out.

Nolan Giles, a fictional character, is a phantom of the young soldier — the idealist who took up the rifle for the Union cause. In writing about him, I have come to know and respect the vast numbers of these men who fought. The regimental histories, memoirs, newspaper accounts, and records crackle with the humor, insight, naiveté, spunk and chivalry of these soldiers — many no more than boys. Qualities that we have lost along the way.

I have tried to present the characters in the most accurate settings possible from the vantage point of a century away. Most of the events — battles, orders, marches, and commanders — portrayed in this book are carefully sketched from accounts from *Official Records* and other historical sources. Of particular help have been the regimental histories of the Fourth, Eighth, and Ninth Ohio, the Seventh and Fourteenth Indiana, the Irish Brigade, the newspapers, and the diaries and letters of the soldiers themselves.

I have tried to be as true to the colorful (and off-color) personalities of these men and events as I could. If I have erred in the results, the fault is my own.

— JHC

Dedicated to
Richard

My Friend. My Husband. My Support.
Because of his love for me, he has been
to more Civil War battlefields than U.S. Grant.

The Redemption Of Corporal Nolan Giles

Jeane Heimberger Candido

I

To Be Opened Upon My Death

His energies flickered and lowered. His soul had begun the long slow retreat. Now he was very tired and surrendered to it. Death was like suffocation...he had felt it many times sweep over the battlefield like a cloud gathering up the souls of the dead. Tonight the feeling was the same, except it was benevolent... patient until he finished this last act of contrition.

The call of alarm! The raw peels of a yammering farm bell. A fire! A summons as compelling as the long roll of the battle drum! Another call, from well beyond the Quinn farm far out on Post Road. Joining the chorus a grim bass to harmonize with the mellow alto of the chimes from the church steeple. A crack of musket fire. A blast from a shot gun! The whoops and cheers of men, intoxicated, delirious rode on the gails of December wind.

He had been lost in the long ago while the planet raced into a new year — a new century. This reluctant passenger be aboard only a short time in this new era.

The old veteran rested his head in his hands. He wanted to pray, but did not know how to even begin. Prayer was a foreign language that he had lost the tongue for. The confession would have to be enough. He read it again:

My Dear Son,

How I love you. My most grievous sin is that I could not be a father to you. This crime is entirely my own. For reasons you could not fathom and I had not the courage to confess, I have long felt unworthy of the blessings I have received at your hands.

1

But as these fires within me die, and in what little time I have left, I must lay before you my crime. I owe you the truth. Your father is a fraud and a murderer...

He pushed the pen away. No more. He knew what the paper said. The old lawyer rubbed his calloused hands, forcing heat into the congealed blood of his fingers. Nolan Giles was barely fifty-six, but did not look it. Not a line creased the sharp blue eyes. Even in the dim firelight, he could have read the paper without glasses. His hair, the sheen of ripe, sun-streaked, corn silk, flowed over the damp white collar. But inside, the soul was wearing out; the mind was bent and the heart, long overburdened with remorse, ached for rest.

Another musket report. The clock rang the first heartbeats of 1900. The world was leaving him behind. He let it go.

Some whiskey would help. He wouldn't be the first soldier who went to headquarters drunk. Yes, by the fire. It was as good a place as any to wait.

Giles creased the paper and set it carefully into the breast pocket of his wool coat and turned up the collar against the draft. Nolan tripped the panel on one of the compartments of the oak catalog desk and pulled an amber bottle from the shadows. Slicing away the seal, he stabbed the blade of his penknife into the cork and twisted. Lightning streaked from his arm to his chest. He gasped but did not give in to it. The old cork gave. He poured two inches into a glass. He inhaled, recoiled, and then sipped. The honey brown liquid glided over his tongue then ignited a flame in his chest like Greek fire. No pretense of social breeding, this was raw, aged, profane dragon spit, moonshine. The mottled label cracked like a dried leaf:

2

See you in Hell!
The Delaware Guards — 4th Ohio

Yes, he was proud of this. In the long, slow hours between battles men with lesser regard for the comforts of their fellowmen wrote letters, memorized testament for their ultimate judgement, or filled journals with verse. The Wee Beasties of Sergeant Solomon Chase's company of tender-aged privates conjured up liquid fire--an anesthetic against the infernal rain, darkness, homesickness and numbing cold on the Union troops in West Virginia. For a leaf of script — officer-rates double — a soldier could purchase the effects that gave testimony to its name "Cannon Shot" slapping a soldier senseless with one gulp. The contraband was protected by officers and enlisted men of the regiment like family jewels against embezzlement or worse — confiscation by the Provost.

The recipe was art in progress — derived mostly of rations and what else the company could scavenge: dehydrated onions, apples, peaches, twisted potatoes, desiccated vegetables, plus remnants from their own haversacks: sauerkraut, half-rotten hard tack, molasses, and sugar. Sergeant Chase, a veteran of the Mexican War and a historian of such important footnotes as moonshine had added a little motivation to the ingredients with a half-ration of lamp oil. The conglomeration was covered over with Tygart River water and a lid was hammered over the barrel to be secreted in the woods to ferment. General Kimball called it West Virginia Tea.

It traveled with the army in two medium-sized barrels still faced with the markings of the U.S. Ordnance Department. For a reasonable percentage of the contents Battery B kept it safe and within easy reach in a battery wagon along with the other explosives of war.

In the spring of 1862, Company C had been sent up to Harpers Ferry and the brew was entrusted to the care of B Company of the Eighth Ohio — a brother regiment. The Confederates struck the 8th at Kernstown and in the emergency of moving men and cannon into line the wagon lay vulnerable in the open. Jackson's cannoneers had gotten a bead on it, sent a shell over, and the wagon went up in a thundering fireball, hollowing out a hole deep enough in the countryside to bury a good-sized horse.

General Kimball, outdistancing his staff rode up to the alarm, sure that a whole regiment had been incinerated by some satanic Tredegar cannon. As the shells roared over their heads like the cries of a mountain cat, soldiers lay dazed but otherwise unharmed.

"God damn!" The general blinked at the vaporous cloud that stung his eyes and reined off to deal with the Confederates.

But battle veterans are ever optimistic that even the best can be bettered. Nolan sent men filtering through the camp for fresh ingredients. To add bouquet he poured tincture of iodine from the surgeon's chest. Logistical innovations were implemented, the elixir was batched in smaller quantities, secreted in the false bottom of several ordnance wagons so that it did not draw attention to itself by sloshing on the march. A casualty or discovery and confiscation would be a minor inconvenience rather than a drought.

Yes, he held the bottle to the firelight, this was one of the few things he was proud of. Giles tossed another swallow back into his throat knowing better than to inhale as it passed from glass to mouth. And it was practical to always drink sitting down.

Giles let the quake settle. Then with the bottle and

glass he rose on unsteady legs and scraped across the plank floor to a chair on the apron of firelight. He eased back in the Windsor back, cupping the right instep around the ankle of his left leg and lifted the dead wood toward the fire.

Nolan measured off the contents of the bottle into one — perhaps two — hours of drinking. Can't predict death, it comes at its own rate. Didn't want to drink too quickly and not have enough for the last minutes or have any left over.

The old friend in the glass drew him back through the blackness of the meanwhile to the immense silent space of his Dublin, raw youth — the cavalier who escaped the back country of Ohio to find the war. He was giddy, young, optimistic, warm again.

Another fleeting alarm stabbed like lightning from his palm to his shoulder and he banished it with another swallow.

II

Giles raised his glass, "To the II Corps and the bad luck of Company C to have led the way!" He let it slide down. With fat, stiff fingers, Nolan pressed the stem of his pocket watch and the golden case sprung open. A tintype had been perfectly sized and secreted into the recess — silver ghosts of two buck privates Nolan Giles and Brian Quinn. Arm in arm they stood flushed with the arrogance of young brigadiers, as green and unbruised as spring apples. Grand Defenders of the Republic, only two of nearly two million, blooming roses. The shorter man could have been the younger of the two, except for the hardness around the eyes as if the soul had already reached manhood before the body. The smile of the other seemed tight on the lips, commanded by an authority outside rather than springing from a spirit within.

Uniforms overpowered their slight frames, the sleeves hiding all but the tips of their fingers. Boys in men's armor. Giles hardly as tall as the bayonet that capped his Enfield, the other about even as they stood at Order Arms.

"Oh, weren't we the dandies lining up at the photogaleria wagon; hardly time to fasten up the buttons before we were pushed in front of the lens." The tired veteran saluted and inhaled another swallow. The fire coughed showering glowing cinders on his boots. He leaned back and allowed himself to remember...

"The President has called for 75,000 men — that's all — and if we don't sign up the war will be over before we can be in it. Sumter is on fire, Congress is calling for blood." At first light, Nolan had ridden out to the Post Road Farm to enlist his friend in his plan, his blue eyes glowing like flames with spirit. "We will go to war before summer sure enough

6

and we got to be already at the head of the line. Why Columbus is already drillin' and the militia will be called up any minute. There won't be but a few openings for us. The way I see it our best option is over in Delaware. Cop Davis said they are signing up volunteers and if we hustle we can get two spots." One of the barn tiger cats shimmied up against his leg. Nolan scooped it up and ran a hand over its back.

"Could be your twin." Quinn smirked. Restraint and caution the best medicine against another of Nolan's passions which blew up as regular as gales in April. To wear down his energies, Quinn handed his friend a hatchet and nodded to the smaller branches of the fallen cherry tree — the ice still glistening in the cold sun. "Kindling." Quinn ordered and resumed his attack on the tree.

"Your mother must have grieved over this. She planted that tree the year my mom..." Nolan brought the blade down and splinters flew like sparks. After a few swings his mind cleared and he took up the cause again.

"Can't wait until planting's done. Don't know when spring's ever getting here...don't show signs of coming soon. The Union needs us now to put the rebellion down." Nolan turned to another branch.

"It's not good that spring's so late." Quinn shivered as black clouds drifted under the sun. As man of the house it had been his responsibility to worry about crops, too much rain, too little rain, too much harvest, and low prices. He had been a man without ever being a boy. His brothers would soon be thirteen, but they were as rowdy as puppies, requiring a firm hand and a vigilant eye. Quinn might never get away.

Brian ran the blade over the sharpening stone and attacked another branch. "Crawford organizing a company you say?"

7

Giles seized the opportunity, "Over at Templar Hall...only takin' 100 men and then they'll be off. Can't wait for another company — might not be time — the war will be over by then."

The gasp might as well have been a thunder clap. Quinn's mother stood in the doorway, cups of steaming coffee held rigidly in her hands. "What is this talk about rebellion? War? No! There will be none of that for my sons."

Giles stuttered; he would not hurt Kathleen to save any cause. This tiny woman had stood against prejudice and starvation and beat them both from her door.

The boy took a deep breath, what to say? The sheep bleated as the collie corralled a new lamb and nudged it back to its mother. The ewe coddled it. These sheep were as precious as currency. From the wool came Kathleen's coverings, shawls, and other weavings, enough income to support her invalid sister, three sons, and a nephew. They — animals and boys — were all Kathleen's lambs. She knew of war and causes — she fought them every day.

He faced her; she must understand, "The President has called for 75,000 troops to take back Fort Sumter. Taking only thirteen thousand from Ohio. We — Brian and I — are thinking of joining up."

"They will do it without my son and without you, Nolan. What would your mother say?"

He did not have to fight the protests of a dead mother, Kathleen was enough. And he wanted her blessing. When his father's madness was too much, sanctuary lay just inside her cabin. To be able to turn the handle of the door without so much as a knock was a privilege he guarded. It was Kathleen who had embraced the unruly boy — coaxing and conjoling a man out of youth. Nolan ached, "My...my mother loved...this country."

8

"Your mother was a Quaker and the daughter of missionaries. She abhorred war, how can you profane her memory with talk of joining it?"

Giles drew back, he shuddered with shame at the tears glistening in the ridges of her cheeks.

"Ma'am, the war is coming, that is sure." Giles took the cups from her trembling hands, and passed one to Quinn without looking in his eyes. "How long it lasts and who wins depends upon who gets there first with the most. If we don't go, some other woman's son will go. It makes no difference, I guess, to the President or the Confederates, but it does to the man who wants to say he was there. To have been a part of something better than plowing, fencing, and fixing. If no one goes, there will be no country for any of us. Isn't that what you came here to escape?"

Kathleen flinched as if she had been slapped. She pulled the corners of her shawl more tightly around her shoulders. "The sons of Ireland lived by the beat of the drum. There was always a cause. Always a fight. I have lost a husband and a father to the cause of a union; hanged by the Queen's soldiers. What good is a union if it costs everything worth living for? When have you paid enough?"

"Ma'am, a man needs something to fight for."

"No, Nolan, he needs something to live for. Someday, you will understand that. Peace is harder on men, but war is harder on women." She turned back into the house.

Quinn growled, "Is it Union you want or to be away from your father?"

"There is every cause. Besides what have we got back here? What have you got back here? Irish isn't prime. How long will it take before you are bated into a fight by a drunk and shot down? If not you then, Ian and James — they're young and don't understand — what in the way of respect do they have to look forward to? Will they have your patience? Will they be able to walk away from the taunts? What life will they have if you don't give these people something to respect?"

The cup trembled in Quinn's hand, as if it were too hot to hold. Nolan relaxed and put an arm on his friend's shoulder, "God knows I wouldn't know respect if it came up and punched me in the jaw. But for what you've done here, you deserve it. Your mother deserves it."

Quinn flushed crimson except for the hair-line seam of white — a scar — a souvenir of one of Giles' Halloween escapades. Funny he should remember now. Old Woman Haskins was greedy with her pumpkins and wielded a squirrel rifle like a Wyandot. The smaller boy had wiggled through the thicket, but Quinn, who had shied from the enterprise in the first place had a tougher squeeze. Kathleen had found them in the barn whimpering, faces and arms scratched, their clothes in shreds as if they had been attacked by bears. After seeing to their wounds she tanned them both and proceeded to give Mrs. Haskins an airing of Irish outrage. Nolan loved her for it.

If Nolan was the nerve, Quinn was the conscience — an odd dependence for a temperance minister's son to make. If Quinn believed the course right, then it must be right, even if he had been brow beaten into going along with it. Nolan needed that permission now. He pressed on, "Besides, do you really think we will have to fight? The Rebs will see us coming and high tail it back into the mountains. Mark my words, you'll be back in Dublin in plenty of time to plant. This war will be over by July at the latest and we'll be back without a scratch, our chest a drippin' with medals from whoppin' the Rebs. And won't Myra be proud!"

Quinn braced; Myra Capwell was a cause to live for,

to draw a man closer to a fireside instead of away from it. The most beautiful woman in Dublin, at least, Franklin County to be sure. A woman who could have any man she wanted — except the son of an Irish rebel. Her father had put a stop to the next unwelcome step and crowded her shadow with a shot gun loaded and at the ready.

"Don't short change the Rebs. I figure they can't be much different than us — just as fired up. I don't think they'll run. If they don't run, and we don't run, we're going to have a hell of a fight."

Giles turned and mounted the little bay, "I'm going home to pack a few things. The stage leaves at four. We can be in Delaware by eight — still should be plenty of time to sign up. War fever is running hot, places be filled quick. No use waiting for the rest of the country to come in and water the war down." Swinging up onto the blanket, he gathered up the reins, "I'm leaving Quinn, with or without you."

"I've got responsibilities."

"The twins can care for your mother. You were younger than them when you picked up the plough. Do them good. Keep them out of trouble. You baby them too much. Wonder what your father would have said."

Quinn's eyes burnished like brass, looking beyond his friend for something only the Irishman could see. Quinn rubbed the white line tracing his jaw. Another prank!

His heart raced. If the old woman meant to scare them, she had achieved her purpose. There were only the two of them, the shells plucking at the thickets behind them. It was an awakening; to be suddenly alive; death whizzing past your ear. It was not Nolan's promise of manhood that tugged at him, but the opportunity to be a boy...

Nolan flicked the reins against the horse's flanks, "They ain't going to hold the train forever."

III

Nolan moved around the black Bible resting on the front table, wary as if it would reach out and grab him. The Testament was a gauntlet slammed down by his father the day Nolan refused baptism. It was as a pointed finger to hell. As long as he did not pick it up, Nolan owned his own soul.

He would not take it with him to war. Instead from under his mattress he pulled a smaller version. He had found it along with an empty locket under his mother's pillow after they had taken her away. He liked this Testament better. The same words, but different gods. Her's a god of love, humor, and forgiveness; his father's a god of damnation and intolerance. His mother's a better companion for whatever comfort he might need on the way.

He thought of her. A picnic by Indian Run, his mother teaching Kathleen some lilt. Quinn had picked it up and whistled it effortlessly, but the notes eluded Nolan like flying soap bubbles. "Simple Gifts" she repeated — a Quaker jig of a song. He was almost in tears when his mother nestled him into the hump of her abdomen, "I think the lad has a tin ear, Kate."

These memories along with the essentials of minimal survival and comfort, he stuffed into the valise. His father's heavy boots pounded on the plank floors of the hall. They stopped in front of his door. The aching hinges whined. Nolan looked up, but went on with his packing.

The black frock coat fell over Martin Giles like a long cassock, eyes of winter-hardened ice framed within thick brows and a full beard as dark as his coat. The two men did not speak, Nolan closed the bag and reached for his coat. His father filled the doorway. His son stopped, held his ground without a flinch.

There were no words left. In the twelve years since his wife's death, they had become foreign to each other. Yet Martin saw in his son the living mirror of his gentle wife, within his grasp but unreachable. He wanted to protect him...to save him...so much of the devil in the world...

"Where are you going this time?"

"Quinn's. Been invited to supper. Staying over." A lie, but a shot in self defense.

"You know I disapprove..."

"I know." Giles turned to pass, but his father cut him off.

"You do it in defiance of me?"

"In defiance, with your blessing, no matter," his son growled. It was a blessing at least that this would be the last time they would have to face each other.

"What is over there that you crave so badly?"

"A family." The truth was a great burden finally unloaded. Was this the man that such a gentle woman could have fallen in love with? Was he conceived in any happiness?

"I forbad it then and I forbid it now!"

The thunder had lost its power on the boy. A lilt was dancing in his brain:

'Tis a gift to be simple, 'tis a gift to be free,
'Tis a gift to come down where you ought to be.
And when we find ourselves in the place just right.
'Twill be in a valley of love and delight."

That was it!

"Answer me, Boy! You don't pray while you are there?"

Nolan startled. The memory shimmered and flickered out. Rage throbbed in his temples. "What?"

"Pray. You don't pray with Catholics!" The vengeance of the Bible in the hall was there again.

The absurdity almost made him laugh, "Pray? No! Heavens, I wouldn't want to pray with Catholics. A crime certainly? We know they don't pray, they conjure! Right, Father? No one sees them, but we all know they do it by their firesides...at midnight...when the moon is full. They call down the Irish witches, fairies, the banshees, and the little people. Rocks rise up, melt and take shape. Clouds swirl into phantoms that move like the angel of death to the doorways of the cursed." His arms swirled, and the reverend recoiled.

"You are afraid of them aren't you, Father?" Nolan hissed. "The Catholics. Or is it the rebel Irish? Or both. Do you think on it at night? That tonight might be the night. A full moon will awaken the madness in their souls — the madness that smolders down in every one of them. Latin chants will roll from their mouths like incantations whirling up to the sky like a tornado — a staircase for the banshees.

"Quinn will rise up as their rightful leader! Father. Have you ever stopped to wonder how many there might be out there? The Quinns are just what we know about, but what about those who have changed their names to escape the prejudice and torture? How many can there be? Enough for a revolution? How many will rise up, strap on their sabers, pull on their armor, and mount their steeds to ride as swift as Pegasus down on the town? Will they be enchanted? Will the hooves pound on the road or will they ride the wisps of clouds, noiselessly? Will you hear them coming in time, Father? Will they come screaming through the town to severe your head as clean as a knife through butter? Or will your neck crack like an ax through kindling? The last satanic scream, the swing of the saber and all is blood."

Nolan sneered. "Worry not. There are no clan sabers

over their mantles, the Quinns are too poor to own a horse, and their farm is so far out Post Road that it would be morning before they could run to town. You had better fear the drunks and rowdies. One of them will likely crack your skull with a rock to steal your wallet or run you over in his wagon without a by-your-leave. But you will rest easy down in your casket, at least they won't be Catholics."

"You will show me respect. I am your Father!" Martin Giles reached for his son as he passed. "You will not go there any longer."

Nolan turned, they stood within inches, Nolan could feel the heat of the man's breath wash over him. Their eyes were level. When had he grown as tall as his father? The realization startled them both. The son turned into the hall, "I will go there whenever I like. And you will allow it. Mother made you promise. And what kind of Baptist would you be if you broke a promise to a dead woman?

"But if you must know the truth I am not going to the Quinn's. I am catching the stage for Delaware."

"What is there, for God's sake?"

"The Army. I am going to join the Army."

The truth struck the preacher as ludicrous. "The Army? What will the Army have to do with you? You are undisciplined, uneducated, without a shred of faith or allegiance to anything in your whole, barren soul."

"Well, if that is so, Father, maybe the Army will do what you and all your Bible posturing could not. Make a man of me."

The cleric took a step and raised a fist over his head, "You blaspheme! Go! But you will be back in shame when the Army will have nothing of you. It cannot ask God's blessing on its cause with the likes of you in its ranks."

Professing a courage he did not have, Nolan kicked

open the door of the cabin and walked out.   The cold wind filled his lungs like resolution.

IV

The stage was nothing more than a springless wagon with two rows of benches anchored behind the driver. Canvas was stretched over a canopy to shield the passengers against the hard conditions of winter travel — rain, snow, wind, mud and manure thrown up from the wheels. Three times per day it left the Black Fox tavern, with passengers, parcels and mail from Columbus for Delaware and connections north. Passengers gathered at the door, four large men — three in the work clothes of sodbusters, the other standing slightly adrift, in the neat frock coat and trousers of a merchant or lawyer. There hardly seemed room for two more, but Nolan had been sold two tickets.

The four large men would make a tight fit, two more would be a squeeze. But human freight offered plenty of muscle to pull the wagon out of the ruts and repair breakdowns that were frequent along the Scioto Stage Road.

The driver wedged the last trunk between the seats and the spare wheel and strapped the load down. The horses tugged to lessen the strain on their harnesses. Passengers started to climb aboard and the driver motioned for the boy to find a seat. Nolan searched down the road that ran between the ribs of barren trees and rough houses. It was empty.

The driver checked the cinches, and pulled the team away from the hitching post. The horses were tired but would last till the swing station at Belle-point where fresh ones would take the stage to Delaware and north.

It was barely dusk but the street already crawled with the usual faithful rushing to Thursday night services held at the numerous saloons. Little more than sheds pulled the farm hands and itinerants to their greasy bars and home-made whiskey. Those with silver in their pockets would test their manhood on the turn of a card. Glasses slammed on the table were quickly refilled; whoops of laughter and vulgar oaths floated out of the open windows like heavy smoke. Those wiser in the way of card sharks kibitz as local boys bet their buckles.

There were more bars in Dublin than any other commerce, the only pastime in the hard-scrabble town. When South Carolina seceded last Christmas the mood had turned ugly. War talk had been nothing new, but now there was venom behind it. As the whiskey flowed, the fires of revenge heated up. In the moonlight the river bank would reverberate with shouts and hoots of men shooting rats named Jefferson Davis, Robert Toombs and Alexander Stevens.

The sun was fading into twilight. His father would be fastening his tie, readying for his holy missions to preach against the damnation of drink. A large congregation tonight.

When he was a boy his father had taken Nolan with him. How the vision still terrified him. The big man framed in the doorway of the tavern, with his Bible raised to call down righteous wrath upon the damnable raving sinners within. He would rant testament until a bunch heaved him back into the street.

"Better get aboard, Son, if you are going." The driver was pulling on heavy gauntlets.

"My friend is not here yet."

"He can catch the morning run. Now, friend." The driver pulled himself up into his seat.

Giles weighed into the coach and the tavern keeper pulled down the flap and secured it. The coach lunged forward as the driver whipped the horses and turned them north, then east across the covered bridge spanning the swirling Scioto. The echoes of the hoofs on the bridge planking echoed back like gun shots. Nolan pulled his collar against the chill. The team turned north running the east side for the long run to Belle-point. The late afternoon twilight was translucent against the muddy gum blanket gaping against the frame. Nolan pushed it open an inch to assure himself that Dublin was actually drifting behind.

The stage bucked and dipped, the holes and gullies pulling and sucking at its steel-rimmed wheels. Passengers wedged into the tiny space bounced and tilted, propelling and catapulting even big men into the air. The winter had been hard on the road, the river overflowed regularly to tear and gouge rifts in the limestone base. When spring was secure street crews dispatched from Sheriff Davis's jail would pound sand and rock back into the crevices.

Nolan was giddy the war came as a liberation, for Quinn a sacrifice. Although he felt like a body adrift without his soul, he did not blame Quinn for remaining.

His brain burned with the flux of his father's threats. He would fail, reveal himself the coward, serve himself up for ridicule and public humiliation. Nolan rocked back in his seat. The stage jerked and stopped. Outside, familiar voices.

The gum blanket was pitched aside and a bundle dropped on his feet. And then Quinn hauled himself up and inside, seating himself on the floor against his friend. "I didn't have enough time to get to town." Nolan grasped his friend's hand.

On the bank, Kathleen Quinn stood rigid; she would not insult them with public tears or sentimentality. The little boys in them might crave it, but the men in them would not forgive the embarrassment. She had accepted the inevitability of another call of the drum and the cause of another union. She waved to them, "Take care of each other. Come home, my sons. Come home when it's over."

"My horse is stabled at the Black Fox. Send Ian and keep him please...for yourself...until we come home. By Independence Day, I promise." Nolan waved.

The driver with no time in his schedule for sentimental leave taking roared, "Aboard!" The coach jerked forward and rolled into the black hollow of the River Road.

The passengers settled off into what sleep could be grasped in their bucking craft. All except the one in the black suit, he had been aroused by Kathleen's brogue and that of the new passenger. He leaned against a corner and pressed a hand over his wallet.

V

Delaware, unlike Dublin, was affluent, cultured, and busy. Of some renown for its health spa and mineral springs, the stores reaching three stories of magnificent brick ornamented with cupolas and balconies. Merchants sold finery and imports that the rough town of Dublin would have little need of.

The stage lunged past Ohio Wesleyan and there was a girls Seminary further off. Nolan wondered of the debates, lectures, mathematical intrigues that went on behind the windows. Lamps burned golden from the rooms of rich men's children who were sent there to learn calculus, Greek, Latin and Shakespeare instead of plowing, milking, and butchering.

For some even this town had even grown too small, one of its sons Rutherford B. Hayes had left for Harvard to study law. He was in partnership with Thomas Sparrow in Columbus. Having all this, who could want for more?

Gas lights lining Sandusky Street flared with the evening gusts. As the stage passed down between them, they quivered and pulsated like summer lightning. Somewhere men were cheering and a band rollicked *Yankee Doodle* with more enthusiasm than talent. The chorus grew louder — something about saving the Union followed by another round of hurrahs. A revival was under full steam. Gun shots, more huzzahs and a waving of torches.

Nolan hung out the stage and watched it all roll by in a delirious succession of delights. How could it have all been so close all this time? He was as euphoric as a prisoner just released from a life's sentence.

The stage reined up. Nolan stepped down and inhaled the giddy night air effervescent and intoxicating. He pulled Quinn toward the band now well into the second verse of

Yankee Doodle. A volunteer waving a long-necked bottle stepped forward to rejuvenate the rhyme with home-spun lyrics.

>The boys of Delaware went to town
>Just to sign the roster.
>To kick the sons of Davis in the uhmm
>And bring old Dixie asunder.

The singer was a tall red-faced boy whose thatch of brick-colored hair overflowed his battered hat like a bush. He bowed and was roundly saluted for his witty couplets with a slap on the back that nearly upended him. The congratulatory bottle was passed like a baton. After two large swallows for inspiration the next singer took up the relay with his own musical assault:

>Lincoln wants 75,000 men
>To make the Rebs po-li-te.
>A Union man 's worth two to one
>Delaware 's all you need to fight.

Nolan shook his head. With another swig, the first man motioned for quiet and pointed for the maestro to strike up a fanfare for a return salvo:

>Jeff Davis rode to Richmond town
>Not to become a resident.
>He wasn't good enough for the army
>So they made him president.

"That's awful!" Quinn groaned.
"It's the thought that counts." Nolan winced.
"Is there thought at work here?" Quinn chuckled.
"My feet smell better than that song!" The tenor

passed the bottle back. "I think you need this!"

"Bravo, Inspired! Simply inspired." Nolan took off his hat and bowed to the troubadours in mock admiration. The two revelers looked up, and bowed likewise.

"Are you believers?" The bigger one in the muddy flannel shirt staggered to within three inches of Quinn's face and hiccuped. "Jamie MacGowan at your service. All Sons of Abraham are welcome to a drink." He stretched out a bottle which Nolan would have grasped if Quinn had not pulled him back.

"Are you crazy? That could be kerosene." Quinn turned to the other local who sat down in the middle of the road when his swaying had made him seasick. "Friend, can you tell me where I may find Templar Hall?"

"Name's Brenton Christie, and what you want is over there!" He pointed with the neck of the bottle. "A. Strauss Clothiers, but don't buy nothin'. Stuffs for lawyers and undertakers. The Army will provide you with a new suit. Better hurry, about filled up the roster, when Mac and me signed up about an hour ago."

"You traveled all the way from sobriety to the farside of purgatory in just one hour?" Quinn whistled in real admiration. "He's got more alcohol in him, than my mother burns in a lamp all winter."

"Thank you, Friend." Nolan moved toward the three-story brick emporium.

"Your obedient servant, I'm sure. After you've been properly baptized in the spirit come out for a liba...liba...for a drink."

The twin gothic doors stood open and the two were given the come on in from inside. Two men sat behind a long table and in front of them rested a large sheet with two rows of signatures, and a couple of ink pens.

A large man wearing a hat with a red plume nestled in the crease of the left brim handed Quinn a pen. Cheeks and jowls sagged on either side of his smile. The brass buttons of his officer's coat pulled under the strain of the barrel stomach. Quinn held the pen aloft wondering if this could be their commander and whether he had garnered those captain's bars in any fight this side of the new testament.

The officer shifted the sheet closer to the recruit and pointed to the second to the last line before Quinn could read the fine print. He smiled as if he were selling ten acres of swamp land. The other, lean and sober as the proverbial judge, stood mute as the captain with the immense epaulets did the selling, "Two fine sons of liberty with the chrism of Bunker Hill on your foreheads. Step this way."

"This must be the place." Nolan slapped his friend on the shoulder.

"Step up and be counted. Delaware is asking you to commit to just ninety days — more than enough to straighten this misunderstanding out. Thirteen dollars per month — the wages of Southern sin."

His associate eyed the two young farmers and handed them a pen. "Can you read and write?"

"Of course." Quinn retorted.

"The man meant nothing by it. Sign." Nolan whispered.

"I want to read it first."

The grim reaper in the black suit regarded the Irishman with some disdain, "Laddie, do you think your government would ever cheat you?"

"This isn't Parliament, Quinn, the man is just trying to help us do what we came here to do."

"Can't place your faces, boys. From around here?" The big recruiter squinted.

"From Dublin," Nolan volunteered as Quinn scowled back. "Hope you won't hold it against us, Sir."

"Not at all." He handed Quinn the pen, and the boy leaned over to sign.

As he did, the other sized up Nolan over his pince-nez, "How old are you, Son?" The clean jaw, the brush of blonde hair, and puffy sleep-filled eyes made Giles look just on the far side of knee pants.

"How old do I have to be?"

"You have to be over eighteen," the Grim Reaper replied.

Just as Quinn had signed away the next ninety days of his life to the government he saw his partner back away.

"Like to read this in the light. Be back presently." Nolan picked up a copy of the Delaware Gazette and moved to the light by the door.

Outside a John the Baptist held the front steps like a pulpit posturing and defaming the Confederates over the insult in Charleston Bay. Few took any notice, choosing rather to toast their patriotism, the cause of the Union, President Lincoln and mother. Nolan watched the revelers hoisting still another toast. The bottles were getting heavier as the men staggered under the weight. At the same time their aim was getting bad, whisky was pouring down their necks and under their collars. Nolan ached to be apart of it.

"Did you sign yet?" Nolan hissed.

"Yes, I signed. You told me to sign." Quinn glowered. "Didn't you sign?"

"Not yet. A complication. He said I have to be eighteen to join."

Quinn's eyes blew up so big that Nolan thought they would pop out of his head. "What are you going to do? You aren't eighteen!"

"In two months I am. It's just a technicality really." Giles watched the one called Mac. He was lying on his back contemplating the stars from his vantage point in the middle of Sandusky Street, pedestrians, horses and wagons milling around him.

"Well, Andrew Jackson in there don't look like he's going to take a down payment on two months. You need to pay up eighteen years right now. And you better think fast, because they own me and the government don't look like they are in the business of refunds."

Nolan waved away his friend's growing apoplectic attack like a pesky mosquito. Up to this point Quinn's conscience was like the North Star, Nolan leaned on it, guided on it like a beacon. Now he found it an inconvenience and wished Quinn would just look the other way. Nolan continued to watch the revelers. He wanted to find out what was in that bottle. Quinn would not let him boldly lie, probably tell on him, have him arrested. Then go marching off without him, win medals, be a hero, and never forgive him for the insult.

Then there was the government. If they found out he wasn't over eighteen...over eighteen...yes, that was what the man said. He had to be over eighteen. Hardly an inconvenience at that.

Nolan tore a strip off a placard A. Strauss Clothiers had nailed to the door. "Fine broad cloth, cashmere suits, pantaloons, and vest of all kinds". Such luxury in a town so close to Dublin where a man rarely wore a suit even to be buried in. A question of good manners that had long troubled him. Why must a man get all fancied up in a suit only to wear it once and then for all eternity be hidden in a casket where no one was going to see it. It's not as if God cared, turn him away from heaven's door for not wearing a tie. Sent us down naked, probably took us back the same way. Brain was rambling. Tired. A debate for another time. But the answer to his current dilemma was about to be solved.

"Got a pencil?" Nolan patted Quinn's chest from which his friend duely extracted a stub. Giles scribbled the magic number 18 on the underside of the scrap of advertisement and folded it in quarters. Hauling off his boot, he dropped the paper down and stuffed his foot back inside. The wad crumpled under his instep and Nolan bounced on it till it was flat. Satisfied, he turned his friend toward the door just as two large men making hell bent for leather turned up the step.

"Naw...that's no better than lying." Quinn hesitated.

"It's fulfilling the terms of a government contract. Now move!"

"I'll sign that paper now, General." Nolan extracted the pen and moved it over the last line at the bottom of the paper.

"You eighteen, Boy?" the official sized him up short.

"Over eighteen, Sir. Well over." Nolan grinned standing straight, handing back the pen.

The official let off a calamitous whoop that rocked even the commotion outside. "We have our company..signed...sealed...and delivered."

"Wait a minute!" the johnny-come-latelys pushed the diminutive recruits out of the way. Looking as immovable as the brick walls around them they stood up to the officials. "We got here as soon as we could. We had orders to fill over at the chair factory."

"Yea!" agreed a grizzled bear of a man in a red wool jacket, the stocking cap pulled down over his forehead. Red-rimmed eyes matching a huge, ruddy nose as large and sharp as an ax head were the only features left naked by a bush of heavy black beard.

The ancient soldier stepped back to let the younger official handle the disturbance, although it was he who was armed with a glistening three-foot presentation sword. The mill worker molded a huge fist and brought it down hard on the table. "We have a right. We live here — born and raised, Delaware tax-payers and all. These guys just got off the stage — heard it said outside. "

"Sorry, Hurse. Comin' as you did, got to take things in order. But the judge is signing up for another company as soon as Governor Dennison gives us the go ahead. You can be the first. Come back in a couple of days."

"Yes," said the grim reaper. "What has been written, has been written!"

The two men closed in for further discussion with the two usurpers, but Quinn pulled Nolan out the door. They were caught in the embraces of the inebriated welcoming committee. Hands were pumped, congratulations passed all around. By now the rest were sufficiently ahead of the two in celebration as to be beyond reach. In a gesture of comradeship Nolan accepted the bottle, wrestling Quinn's hand from its neck, hoisted it in salute to the flag snapping over the entrance.

Barely a drop touched his lips, the alcohol flowed like a waterfall down his neck and into his shirt. The man called Hurse had hoisted the little recruit off his feet and was shaking him until his head bobbed. Nolan winced at the hot vinegar exhaled in his face, "You are going in there and resign or you are going to be the first casualty of the war."

"Now, Horse. I believe that was your name. You must be a good sport about this."

"Hurse!"

The revelers rushed forward as fast as their unsteady

legs could go and grabbed at the millwright's sleeve. Nothing budged. "Put him down. That ain't polite." Christie seethed.

"Yea," Mac swayed as if the effort of the one word was enough to knock him off balance. "There will be plenty of rebs left over for another company. Let him go."

"Good advice." Nolan gasped, he was sinking out of his coat.

"Let him go. Sign up with the new company. Probably make you captain." Quinn pulled at the man's sleeve.

"Or the pack mule." Nolan did not know where that came from. It sounded like his own voice, but he had never before been so intemperate as to poke a stick into the eye of a rattlesnake.

"What did you say, John Hancock?"

Quinn stepped closer and Horse's associate from the chair factory closed in. One of the drunken company stepped up to mediate, but tripped on his shadow, throwing Nolan into Horse's fist which was at ready fire only an inch from the target's face. The four ricocheted off each other and the candle went out in Nolan's cranium.

In the haze, there was a ringing in his ears and yet another verse of *Yankee Doodle*. Bodies churned, rocked, and grabbed for balance before re-entering the fray. As word traveled down the street that the company was already engaged in its first skirmish, men emptied out of the buildings to take up the cause without asking as to the particulars of disagreement. As bodies flew, it became difficult for the fighters — let alone the reinforcements — to remember who was enemy and who was friend. The cause disintegrated into a general free-for-all.

Horse had discarded Nolan to take on Quinn. President Lincoln's newest son rolled over to the curb; the whiff of manure stung his nostrils. A fresh heap lay just an inch from his face. It cleared his brain abruptly and Nolan pulled himself up unsteadily, turning just in time to see his best friend's face receive the full force of Horse's meteor fist. He winced, Quinn brought up a rapid punch before a swirling galaxy of stars could ruin his aim.

A fraternity brother tripped the big laborer and he fell back like a building. The forces of the Delaware Guards were about to declare victory against tyranny when the local constabulary called a cease fire. Two against six had been an unfair fight in any man's book. And from the looks of them, it was past time for the law to come and save the six from annihilation before they were too banged up to go off and annihilate the enemy.

"All right. All right." A tall, powerful man and two assistants strolled into the melee, pulling men free of each other. The man with a brass shield on his shirt took inventory and turned to the two strangers. "What's going on here?"

"Just a difference of opinion, Sir." It didn't take much of a prophet for Quinn to see they just might be spending their first night in a Delaware jail.

"Looks like a clear case of drunken and disorderly." The deputy moved from one casualty to another searching the pickled soldiers for prospective borders for the night. He recoiled when he got down to the poet. "God, Christie, I ain't even going to arrest you. Your mother will fix you?"

"No," Christie rose to his own defense. "It was an accident. Horse and Johnson. I mean Hurse, here...Sir. The Mick is right. Just a misunderstanding, Marshal." Christie belched the exhaust of several bottles of corn whiskey into the deputy's face. Nolan put his head closer to the discussion so he could hear over the intense pealing of bells that rocked inside his brain.

Christie took up the cause again, "Horse and Johnson, you see, just fell down some stairs. That's how he bloodied his nose, you see. Clear case of miscalculation. We was just helpin' him up."

Quinn rubbed his bleeding lip, "Daniel Webster here is going to get us thirty days just for insulting an officer's intelligence." But Nolan let him plead their defence, the officer and the townie had obviously had a long history.

"Christie, you wouldn't be haulin' me any of your bull?"

"Marshal, I'm a duly-sworn defender of the Union. Doubting me is like doubting Abraham Lincoln. Look, Sir, you take charge of the two Horses of the Apocalypse there, and we'll take our brethren and retire. Peacefully."

"Well, just get off the streets before you get run over! Go on." The Marshall gathered up the two big men. "Heaven help the Union with the likes of you defending it. At least you will be out of my hair."

"Wait here, Marshal!" Hurse stepped up to the officer to protest.

"Go home...now!" clipped the officer. "Now!" Hurse surrendered to authority, turned his friend and motioned towards home.

The man called Christie snapped a salute and spun around and would have fallen on his face if Nolan and Quinn hadn't netted him between them.

Christie smelled of the manure encrusted to his jacket. The full weight of his predicament began to sink in. "My mother is going to be real unreasonable about this. Do you think she will guess I was in a fight? God, she works up a fury when I've been fightin'. You guys got to stand by me. What a rage when she gets mad. Maybe she won't notice."

"Naw, how could she know?" Quinn straightened the

scraps of the boy's jacket. "Naw, she'll never be able to tell."

"Good." Christie felt better and shuffled between the two.

Quinn licked the blood away from his split lip. It ran like red syrup down his coat and pooled in the holes where two buttons had been ripped away. He ran his tongue over the cut and winced. Tomorrow it would be as big as a mouse. Yes, his mother would be most impressed. Nolan had promised excitement and he did come through on that bill.

"You'll stand up for me?" Christie was babbling like a condemned man as the four stumbled up the steps of the little cottage. The three other God-fearing Christians nodded. Christie understood better than the rest that in the face of the righteous wrath of Widow Christie, God was the lesser of their problems. His new friends promised supporting testimony to any story Christie gave. Although Quinn suggested pleading temporary insanity might save them a lot of time, the others agreed that a bold-faced lie was the wiser course.

"Four against one. Good odds you'd think?" Nolan reassured himself, how bad could it be?

Quinn winced, knowing something about the wrath of mothers, he doubted if they were even as good as the ones they had just left in the street.

Company C
Camp Jackson
28 April, 1861

Myra,

Hooray for Delaware! We formed two companies, but if we had wanted we could have marched two or even three times that. So great was the rally of men to sign up. We are an odd sort of brothers — gentlemen of the highest caliber — most bein' a few years older than me. Farmers most of all, some mechanics, tradesmen and merchants, a few rich boys — they being officers — but those in the ranks just plain scrabble.

Want you not to worry about us. Things have proceeded quietly and without any commotion. Nolan has been most temperate. I think the experience matures him. Your fears about his hot headedness have proved unfounded, he has shown himself to be a most deliberate, cautious fellow.

How you would have loved Delaware! Buildings lining the sides of the street like the ramparts of the old castles my mother used to speak of. The stores are full of dresses, goods, men's suits. Never saw so many men in suits — judges, merchants — look all very prosperous and dress so during the week. They have all been friendly and seen to our care.

We elected a name for our company, I guess it's tradition. We are the Delaware Guards. We elected James Crawford captain and he was the first commissioned by Governor Dennison. Doesn't have any fighting experience that I know. We got enough first and second lieutenants — elected too by the men for reasons other than military experience. I guess the practice of popular vote is traditional, commissions given to anybody who can raise up enough men or is somebody is the community the men will listen to.

Personally I would have liked an officer who had some experience in the business we are about to undertake. It would seem about as important as hiring an experienced surgeon. Before he cuts, I'd like to have the comfort knowin' he ain't learnin' his job as he goes along.

We had a little more than a week off after the company was signed, sealed, and delivered. Nolan and me remained in town. I would so much have wanted to see you again and soothe Mother, but I'd rather not open that vein again. So with so many jobs for strong backs, we empty pockets found plenty of work. I sent Mother the money we got working for Judge Jones and Judge Powell — keeping the fireplaces clean and burning at the Court House.

Marshall Case who was of most hospitable assistance the evening of our arrival, chipped in two bits a day to keep the jail tidy. Being that it's right behind the Court House, it was no bother. But Mrs. Christie, the mother of a carpenter and gentleman acquaintance made upon our arrival — a poet of some repute — had graciously provided us shelter and comforts at no cost. To tell the truth, Myra, the Union Army missed a fine general, restricting enlistment to men. If that woman could swear, Lincoln would have skipped the other particulars and given her a company, so great is her talent to keep men moving. In a matter of days we chopped enough wood to heat her tiny cottage through an eternity of winters, stripped and shingled the roof, painted her house two coats front and back, and walled up the root cellar. The call of war was a welcome relief.

The company just set off the train here at the Insane Asylum, where we will be staying until Camp Jackson across the river is ready to receive us. Columbus is overflowing with men from all over — Marion, Mount Vernon, Canton.

Two regiments are already to move out for Washington. We think we will be the third or fourth.

I do not know from day to day when we will leave for the fight. Although it is blasphemy to say, I don't think we will have to fight. This thing will wear itself out, reasonable men will prevail before violence flares. Nolan and I, being smaller than most, will be well back in the line — two small saplings in a forest of heroes.

I pray that you are well and although I am here, I am always with you. In the future all letters will be posted in care of Nolan and address yours to the same, in that your father would be most indisposed on receiving correspondence from me.

Quinn

VI

"Better not eat that." Mac warned, "Give you worms."

"No self respecting worm is up this early in the spring." Worms or not, the apple, which still puckered with its withered blossom was as hard as rock and Christie threw it into the cook pot.

Camp Jackson, which nestled on the eastern upriver shore of the Olentangy-Scioto confluence, had a number of cook tents to serve the men nourishment--hot which by no means meant cooked, tasty which by no means meant delicious, and plentiful which was by no means meant distinguished for its variety. Although fires were discouraged, the huge Sibley tents were equipped with stoves to keep recruits warm. But a man's spirit still craved a fireside and his stomach home cooking. Although the army was richly blessed in soldiers it was woefully inequipped with cooks. So the men experimented in those domestic tasks which they had taken so for granted at home. And they found the results disagreeable.

After a camp breakfast of hard bread and weak coffee in the mess tent, the little Scot had set his mind to at least improve the culinary lot of their small group. Believing that proficiency in anything began in learning the fundamentals, he put a bucket of water over a fire to boil. Produce scavaged from behind the mess tent was added and he christened it soup. Hope dimmed as friends tested the churning mush boiling up in the bucket. They added onions, sweet potatoes, turnips, and "horse" — the hard meat served up at the Army table. As it boiled up its peculiar aroma the men moved further and further away from the fire.

Mac added a little more salt, let the contents simmer

and pulled a copy of the *Democratic Standard* from his back pocket. It had become the newspaper the boys had come to prefer over the *Delaware Gazette* in that the latter had mixed up the officer's names in reporting the organization of the two companies. Besides George Staymen, the editor of the *Standard* had devoted ink enough for a whole column to include the names of every soldier in both companies and went a long way toward spelling them correctly. He had wound up the story with a footnote, "A strong effort was made to divide our boys in order to provide places for several aspiring gentlemen, who have just about as much knowledge of military affairs as a hog has of preaching." An editor like that deserved loyalty.

Quinn nodded. "The man belongs in office."

"Are you going to start up again?" Nolan shook his head. Quinn had been expounding on the subject of military leadership. "You going to get yourself shot for sedition."

"A man's got a right to free speech."

"You ain't no man, you're a soldier, bought and paid for."

Christie took the paper and turned the leaf, "Another letter from Corporal Warner bringing the homefolk up to date. Yep, there's one from Lieutenant Jones in the *Gazette*. Good boys."

"Reminding them that we need to be kept fed, you mean." Mac sniffed. "About time for some food wagons, we don't belong to the government yet. Damm! Here comes the rain!"

During the last week of April, Quinn and Nolan watched their company become a small spoke in an ever-enlarging wheel. With nine more companies they would form a regiment commissioned by the Governor as the Fourth Ohio Volunteer Infantry. All tolled, Ohio would send nearly two hundred regiments to the war.

Trains arrived daily with companies of men harvested from Ohio cities and farms — too many for the Camp to hold. Camp Jackson had not enough land to hold the reservoir of men that flowed into it daily. Too crowded for drill, the wheat fields churned into swamps from minimal traffic. Incessant rains kept the men inside leaky tents, which accommodated twelve, but now slept as many as twenty — "as crowded as triplets in a womb" Christie grumbled.

The nights were wet and cold but wood floors in tents were considered unhealthy. Camp fever and measles took their toll. Men slept huddled spoon fashion around the center post. When one turned over the rest followed around until all were facing in the same direction. The result, idle soldiers doing what soldiers have done from time immemorial — developing their facility for complaining.

Five days of misery is more than enough time for temporary insanity to right itself. The fire that motivated some men to forsake family, home-cooked meals, and warm beds to live as close as body and soul to the next man, relieve himself in ditches called sinks, live in muddy, leaky tents, eat army cooking which one soldier described as agreeable as charred pine, can explainably cool. A few were even motivated to leave without the formality of permission. With prompt justice, deserters who wanted to go home were often afforded their desire. With heads shaved they were drummed ceremoniously out of the army, the humiliation permanently affixed to their records.

Quinn, Nolan, Brent Christie and Jamie MacGowan — brothers in arms since their first battle on Sandusky Street — melted into the throng of recruits optimistic that great events teemed just beyond the horizon.

Of more immediate interest was Columbus, with the

dome of the state capitol, tall buildings hinting at commerce, activity and enterprise reaching out in every direction. It called to the damp, bored and butt-sore. In spite of the guards, sightseers leaked out of camp to inspect the capital nestled along the Great National Road.

The capitol building teamed with more soldiers, just as bored and butt-sore but enjoying a dryer camp under the rotunda. Threading among prone bodies and mountains of gear, the four wandered the halls peering into offices, inspecting every civilian in a black frock coat wondering what a Governor looked like. Any soldier sporting the black, high-crowned Hardee hat and shoulderstraps might be their new commander, George McClellan. He was the subject on everyone's mind and the papers expounded his biography at length.

The particulars were impressive. Engineer from West Point gone on to some distinction as president of the Ohio and Mississippi Railroads. Before that as vice president of the Illinois Central he had garnered the notice of their chief counsel Abraham Lincoln. Mac, a Pennsylvania man having been appointed head of Ohio Volunteers, struck Nolan as an insult, "Seems like we should have somebody right here at home that's just as good. Only fitting to keep it in the family so to speak. There's Rosecrans from Delaware and Sheridan from Somerset."

"I just want him to have some fighting experience?" Quinn scanned an issue of *The Ohio State Journal* he had found lying under a bench. "Here it is...McClellan...says he won two brevets in the Mexican War."

"Anything in there about where we can get a bite to eat in this town?" Mac peered over Quinn's shoulder.

"What's a brevet?" Christie hoped to be impressed.

"Danged if I know. Medal maybe." Quinn scanned the

ads nestled side by side with the editorials in long black columns of print. The suggestion of food was timely. He was hungry.

"What's a brevet, Professor Giles, a short speech...a small hat?" Christie slapped his friend on the back.

"It's a battlefield promotion. What else does it say?"

Quinn beamed with admiration. That Nolan knew anything more about the army than the location of the company cook tent was a revelation. He went on, "Says he was an observer in the Crimean War."

"Uh huh!" Christie sounded skeptical.

"Now don't be judging the man before he gets a chance to prove himself." Nolan grimaced as drops of rain spotted his faded jacket.Quinn sniffed. Blasted rain, a man can't even read the paper without it turnin' to paste. Nothing but rain and its best friends wind and mud rolling under the tent, seeping into a man's ears and down his neck. Make even a Christian cantankerous.

"Trouble is," Quinn was back on his favorite subject, "This McClellan will be provin' himself with us. If he makes a mistake, well, he'll be the one on the fast horse. We are the infantry I might remind you. Tells you something about our options. Makes you stop and think, don't it?"

"You gotta have faith that the government knows what it's doing? Done it before in Mexico. And got us this far." Nolan put his arm around his friend.

"And where is that? Camp Jackson is truly first class accommodations." Christie pulled his cap down over his head against the rain.

Along State Street men and women packed into the horsecars or ran to the tea rooms and stores — small wings of water rising up under their feet. The boys pulled open one of the capitol's heavy doors and pressed through it to get out of the rain.

"Excuse me." The four breached the doorway just as a slight man nearly hidden under the broad felt hat and yards of blue wool was exiting.

"Are you alright, Sir?" They righted him.

"Oh?" A gale ripped the old relic from his sandy brown hair and sent it flying like a huge black crow toward the capitol horse trough.

Quinn returned molding the black felt back into shape. "I am sorry, Sir." The man accepted the gracious effort and pressed it back on his head.

"Thank you, but I think it's beyond help." He was hunched, languid and deliberate rather than slow of speech. But the eyes — the blue of stain glass when the bright sun shines behind it — took them in.

"It's my fault. Let me buy you another, Mr..." If a matter of honor necessitated Quinn walking back to camp...well, the rest dove into their pockets to pull together the price of a replacement.

The stranger pressed the hat down so not to loose it again. "Grant. Sam Grant. Naw, Son, It's a relic...like me...both of us beyond salvaging it seems." He touched the brim before descending down the cascade of steps out into the driving rain.

Christie watched the man go. "You don't think he's a general?"

Alarm cracked into smiles as his friends warmed to the joke. Quinn shook away their cynicism, "Well, he's wearing a military coat. Mexican War...he's that old."

The lads looked back but the man had already been swallowed up in the street traffic. "Naw," Nolan shook his head, "Don't look like much of a general to me. Better get back. None of us is going to make general either if we are all shot for deserters."

41

Company C, Fourth Ohio Volunteers
Camp Dennison
4 May, 1861

Myra,

We are now a regiment strong — the Fourth OVI — down here at Camp Dennison in Cincinnati (yes, we are seeing the world one step at a time). We have moved into the School of the Soldier. To lead us in our instruction we are fortunate to have the services of the right-honorable Sergeant-Major Solomon Michael Chase, imported from Ulster and cured fifteen years in the Regular Army pickle barrel. Yes, my dear Myra, your emerald-green soldier is in the hands of an Orange sergeant, won't that be a cotillion?

This Dublin philosopher is of the opinion the army picks sergeants for their hatred of the human race--and we are lucky enough to have a sergeant with a blood feud several generations long. So we will be more afraid of him than the enemy. Chase has set us to work with a passion right facing, left facing, about facing, by squad, by file, and every wig wag and zig zag direction that the Army can think of. We look like a ladies' dance class. We drill in the morning before breakfast, after breakfast, before and after lunch, before supper, after, before we go to sleep and in our sleep. In the morning I'm winded before I start.

It will impress you to no end to know that Nolan has been selected as an example, so great did he impress the Sergeant-Major with his potential. Chase is in a hurry up to get us regulation perfect because he is afraid our three-month enlistments will ring up before we can learn the army two-step.

I still breathe the hope that this misunderstanding will be settled before someone is killed. Then there will be no

42

turning back. Men value peace too little. The clasp of your hand, the cry of our child, the pride of an apple picked from our trees is what I dream of and they are worth more than medals to me.

Quinn

VII

"Do you think Sergeant-Major Chase had a mother?" Giles snickered. Like God, Sergeant-Majors see all.

"Boyo," Chase bellowed, "You have something to say?"

Giles braced, "No, Sir."

"Well, the only one bein' paid to talk is me and the only one who knows what he's talking about is me. That don't leave much for you, now does it?"

Sergeants were like rocks it was hard to tell how old they were by just looking. Chase was tall. All sergeants scraped the clouds, and spare, his limbs hanging at regulation sharp angles. His face was tanned, weather-beaten leather a well disciplined mustache hung over a firm mouth. His jaw was square without the beard sported by other regulars. The perennial forage cap topped a ring of black hair trimmed tight against the nap of his neck. His tunic hung from broad, square shoulders and tapered to the waist in folds under a waist belt that glistened like patent leather. Three, blue chevrons crowned by three rockers slashed both sleeves, four brass buttons gleamed fore and aft the breast plate. He looked so at home in Union blue, Sergeant Chase might have been christened in it. He would certainly die and be buried in it and he would be regulation perfect whenever that might happen.

Camp Dennison had a legion of these granite-jawed non-coms with U.S. Army branded on their backsides. They always marched never walked, barked — always with the accent on the last syllable — instead of talked, and drew renewed energy from other men's exhaustion. They were the backbone of a good command, a good sergeant could make or break an officer; a smart volunteer officer knew it, and prized a good sergant to the point of deferring to him.

When Sumter fell, these archangels were called out of the biplaces and back country of the frontier to train civilians — a disdainful task. A good number of them were Irish, brogue still tight about the tongue, but Americans to their heart. It was the Army that gave them not only a life but a living and stature. They weren't going to let a train-load of slack-spine recruits make them look bad in front of the general let alone the enemy.

"Old Sergeants never die. God ain't going to let a man like Chase die and move in on the management of heaven. Likes running things himself." Nolan murmured.

"Easy, Nolan." Christie hissed two men to the left. "Word is Chase fought Indians on the plains."

"Pity the Indians."

The company counted off and broke down into squads for instruction. Providence winked and the four were among the ten damned "Chase's Chosen".

"We'll pray for you." snickered the others as they shuffled off.

Such began the School of the Soldier, preliminary to School of the Company, and School of the Battalion and so on up the line.

The boys looked up to the faded denim blue skies, prayed for rain, but the May sun beat down hot. Maybe it just seemed unusually warm as Chase pulled his little squad up into two ranks thirteen inches between them.

"First, me lads, you are going to learn how to stand. Yes, boys, the Army in its infinite wisdom has a way for everything and there is a way to stand. So starting at the beginning we are going to learn to stand as the Army deems fit and proper. Then we will take up the manual of arms. And if the war is not over, we will learn to march by the front, by the flank, and all the possible combinations that will put us in line without running into ourselves, our officers, knock over the cannon, or the enemy. So to begin, now, do we have any volunteers to help me demonstrate?"

Men stood like statues every eyelash in tight control. "Humble patriots every one. of you, I can see. Well, no matter. Chuckles, yes, you, Mr. Giles, with the runnin' commentary, step forward. So gracious of you to volunteer."

The order ran through his ear canals like a bullet through a rifle barrel, crashed into his brain, and damned up there instead of traveling down his legs. He stood paralyzed below the waist, growing into the parade ground like a tree.

"Now, Mr. Giles, if your please." The earth hiccuped, or more likely Quinn saved his friend from being shot for insubordination by kicking him forward. Either way Giles tipped to the front of the line only inches from the nose of the Sergeant-Major and the precipice of hell.

The instructor stepped behind his victim, the voice of command boomming in his ears. "Now see here, Lads, we have a recruit who can't stand. Oh, he is up perpendicular off the ground to be sure, but the secret is to be able to stand and stand alert for hours — even days. It is the pre-requisite to turnin' over the feet on the long march. That will be your specialty, Lads, marching because you are the infantry. The backbone of the Army — the mudsills — the bottom log between the cabin and the ground. We are not the brains mind you. Them's the engineers who commute directly with God and generals which are interchangeable as far as you are concerned. Then's the artillery. They ride too. And the Quartermaster and Ordnance. Rations, cannon and ammunition ride the wagons and trains, and officers ride the horses. It leaves the only other conveyance sanctioned by the Army to us, sole leather.

"Now," Chase inched so close to Giles' he could feel the heat of the man radiating against his back. "We are going to learn the Position of the Soldier. Heels not quite together on the same line near but not touching," Chase kicked a black toe against Nolan ankles and kept hammering them apart until the recruit's feet spread into an open V stance acceptable to Chase's standards. Nolan lurched but caught himself before he tripped. Then the non-com walked to the front of his victim, and fixed on the squad. Nolan did not blink holding himself as if his spine were a flag pole. His soul and mind were detached from his body and beyond abuse. He had not learned that in the Army, but at his father's table.

"Fine. To continue working up from bottom to top so to speak. The knees are straight but without stiffness." Chase knifed the back of his hand into the back of Giles legs, nearly folding him up onto the ground. "The hips are inclined forward." Chase placed his hands on the thighs and pitched the boy so. Nolan shuffled but caught himself before falling. Chase sighed. "God damn, now we will have to start over. No matter to review."

Chase gripped, shuffled and twisted Nolan churning up a mushroom cloud of dust. Finally to where he had left off, the Sergeant-Major lifted Nolan by the shoulders, "The shoulders are square and sloping but identical on each side. He shimmied them into form and Nolan braced to keep his head from bobbing. "The arms hang naturally, the elbows near the body." Chase slapped the boys palms against his trouser seams. "The palms of the hand turned a little to the front, the little fingers behind the seams of the pantaloons. Perfect."

Chase turned to inspect his work. Close up Chase's eyes burnished like the brass on his coat — clouded though they were beneath the shade of his visor. They radiated authority but not bare-knuckles condescension. Nolan swallowed, why the Sergeant had been testing him!

Nolan fixed forward and Chase continued, his directions ringing like rifle reports. "The head is erect and square to the front. The chin will be near the throat, the eyes fixed forward in a straight line to the ground about fifteen paces ahead. On the march all you will see lads is the back of your friend's shoulders and you will guide on the elbow next to yours and the file closers. Those are the sergeants and lieutenants, your shepherds so to speak. We will be to the right of the column so as you don't wonder off and get lost."

Chase inspected his work, "Comfortable, Lad? Sure you are. The manual says you are." Nolan was feeling a little like a marionette with slack in his strings. Hardly comfortable, but he was not going to tell the Sergeant-Major and break his heart.

"Now, boys that is our lesson for today. Let us give it a little practice. Mr. Giles, you may step back with your mates to practice your listening."

Years later, Nolan came by a worn copy of *Wilson's United States Infantry Tactics and Manoeuvres of the United States Infantry, Including Infantry of the Line, Light Infantry, and Riflemen.* On page twenty-three, paragraph seventy three, it clearly stated, "The instructor allows the men to rest at the end of each part of the lessons, and oftener, if he thinks proper, especially at the commencement; for this purpose he commands REST." Chase must not have thought it proper, fearing that a rest of even two consecutive minutes, would be overlong, allowing the instruction to get lost in the brain.

Sergeant Chase worked them at it a chapter at a time, day after day, until each maneuver was executed by reflex, automatically yet by the numbers with snap and polish. It was all quite simple — elegant really. If a man could count to two — him and his pard and always step off with his left foot he was Army material. They always stood in two lines whether in section, company or regiment. A soldier and the man behind him constituted a file. If you were wounded or killed, it was the Army's supreme hope that the man behind you also was a casualty so that the lines still came out even. The Army disdained ragged lines.

Between bouts of rain the men right faced and left faced until they were dizzy. They mastered the Principles of the Direct Step — marching in common time ninety steps to the minute. When they were exhausted Chase took particular pleasure in introducing the Double Quick Step. Instinctively the veteran could gage the prerequisite one hundred sixty-five steps — not one hundred sixty-six — and not one hundred sixty-four — only that number the Army saw fit as "Double Time" and that number only.

"You're runnin', Lads. No! No! Halt, You, Slack-legged..." A .69 caliber profanity shot through the ranks. "Come back here and we'll do it again."

As they became more proficient sections were grouped until they were drilling by company and then by regiment. Maneuvers became more complex such as converting from rank into marching by a column of fours. And then it was moving from a column of fours into a battle line. There was the cautious maneuver of skirmishing and falling back. All this Sergeant-Major Chase taught with the infinite "patience" famous for the Army non-com.

They were coming along nicely; Chase nodded but did not smile. When his ducks marched with enough competence that they did not embarrass him too greatly in front of the other sergeants Chase attacked the "Manual of Arms". In their sleep recruits garbled, "Shoulder Arms!"

"Order Arms! " repeating the nine-step process that Chase drilled until their fingers were blistered.

Chase owned their souls. Four times a day men moved to the bark of orders until they did not have to think — their feet obeyed long after their brains had gone to sleep. By taps soldiers dropped into their tents too exhausted to remove their shoes. "We could have marched all the way to the Confederate Capital, hanged that son-of-gun Davis, and been back in time for supper." Christie moaned.

"I have the notion that old coot has been in battle before. Knows something about war to live this long."

"Quinn, the eternal optimist. If he's wrong I want my money back." Christie began to snore.

C Company showed the greatest promise, they had become indeed Chase's Chosen — his pets and he rewarded them with longer drill and bluer language. Yes, the boys were coming along...listening up real good. The little blonde with the mouth had something special, didn't cowar, sensed something about the business of war, didn't addle, kept his head, good under fire. Worth watchin' here, might make a sergeant if he weren't careful. One problem, the boy was slow, dense, couldn't yet tell the time by the fife.

From five in the morning till nine at night the drum and fife marched to the center of the camp to call what was next on the schedule. Each call was specific to the task: first call, reveille, breakfast, fatigue, officers call, surgeon's call, drill, recall from drill, first sergeant for guard, guard trooping, adjutant's call, squad drill, recall from drill again, recall from fatigue, first sergeants call again, drummers call, fatigue call, officers drill, dinner call, recall from drill, squad drill, recall from drill, recall from fatigue, retreat, tattoo and taps. The drums and fifes called them all.

Eternally the fifes and drums were ringing orders

down around Nolan's ears. The drums he heard fine, the fifes were like the shrieks of soaring falcons evaporating into a whisper beyond the range of his ears. How could he learn the calls if he could not hear them?

"Don't you know where you're going, Boy?" Chase boomed as Giles was heading off to the mess, his stomach growling louder than the bass drum. "It's fatigue the fifes are blowing. You should know them by now, Lad. Are you slow? Better learn them or you'll be ricocheting off your partners. Get them down pat."

"You're tone deaf, Nolan." Quinn and Mac strode up between their battered friend. "On your own, you're a rudderless boat under full sail."

Quinn put a reassuring arm on his pard's shoulder, "If we don't figure something out somehow, Sergeant Chase will eat you up and spit out only the buttons."

Giles slumped back against the ground. He could see it now, about facing, drilling, manual of arms — all for nothing — drummed out of the Army on charges of tone deafness.

"If you can't hear the fife, you can hear the drum. We'll practice on the cook pot until the drum beat is as familiar as you heart. Anyway one of us will stay as close as your guardian angel." Christie slapped his back.

Salvation came with the introduction of the bugle, a coil of brass used by the British hunters to command their dogs. If a hunting hound was smart enough to recognize different bugle commands, so could a trooper. Wellington proved it, even Julius Caesar had proved it. If the bugle was good enough for Julius Caesar, it was good enough for the U.S. Army.

"I just hope when we got all this down pat there will be some enemy left to fight." Nolan pulled his Brogans back over throbbing blisters to the call of the Assembly.

VIII

It was the mission of Colonel George A. Porterfield, Confederate States of America, to make Nolan's wish come true. But even colonels have their problems. If God had created the universe out of nothing in six days, the newly-established Confederate government at Richmond was prepared at least to be more compassionate. In its benevolence it had granted Porterfield perhaps twice that long to create a Confederate stronghold in the western counties of Virginia. It would take something like a miracle. Wood, Ritchie, Jackson, Tyler, Marion, Lewis, Barbour, Upsher and their neighboring counties had voted against the rest of Virginia defeating the first ordinance of secession that spring. A second note had been called in secret without notifying the troublesome holdouts and it passed April seventeenth. The western counties were of Union sentiment made up of small farmers and merchants mostly, men of disciplined mind and hard muscle, exacting modest yields out of primeval hillsides and twisting valleys. They were not men to be trifled with and when they realized they had been defrauded by eastern planters the angry talk was of seceding from the seceded state.

They were about forming their counties into a resistance and even a state of their own under the leadership of the thorny Francis H. Pierpont when Porterfield arrived in Grafton. Porterfield was to break this Union sentiment by organized military force if necessary, with companies recruited from local manpower. Richmond was optimistic, certainly there were enough patriots in the region to check the rebellion. It was still Virginia after all.

With several companies made up of local citizens Porterfield could then hold the Ohio River and the Baltimore

& Ohio Railroad. The Railroad was vital. It snaked northwest from Baltimore, Maryland, through the disgruntled counties by way of Grafton and Parkersburg. From there the ribbon of steel moved into Wheeling and into the heartland of the Union. The side who had the B&O and unimpeded access of the Ohio River all the way to the Mississippi had a tourniquet on the artery of its enemy.

Richmond had sent Porterfield no staff, supplies, or cannon. But the Colonel was a man of great faith, energy, and enough vanity to think he might pull it off with a brigadier's star in the bargain.

On May 4, Porterfield stepped down from the train at the Grafton station. The officer had waited until all of his fellow passengers had disembarked before making his grand entrance. He smoothed his hair and straightened his uniform, then looked out the window. The officer was annoyed, the station was empty. He had expected, if not a band, at least some small welcoming party of loyal dignitaries to meet him. And where was his army?

A bad omen. The Colonel stretched his legs, and surveyed the wild country. Here nature was loud and impatient. Beyond the tracks, the Tygart River swelled and churned with the interminable spring rains; the winds swirled through the valley, and produced a roar of agitation that never subsided.

The other passengers had moved on to their business, and the rail yard was vacant except for station workers loading the cars.

"Can you tell me where I am?"

A laborer stopped and regarded the stranger with some annoyance. Absently the man pointed to the sign hanging from the awning: GRAFTON.

Porterfield picked up his valise and walked closer to

the man. Discretely he asked information of Confederate troops that might be located in the vicinity. "Don't know nothin' about troops, but there was a rumor that there were fellows waitin' at Fetterman to enlist in the Southern Army." The Colonel nodded, the word "army" made him feel better.

The local regarded the officer's neat, gray, wool uniform, and wondered as to whether the soldier might have better exercised a little sensible discretion and made his entrance a little more nondescript. Union societies teemed through the hills as thick and mean as rattlesnakes, no use poking a stick in their eye, so to speak.

"If you aim to go to Fetterman I'd go quickly if I were you. There are a power of folks around Grafton that's stirred against you fellows. Better rent a horse at the livery stable. It's a two mile trek and with the rains it will be a hard one to walk. Take the Post Road north. Follows the railroad. You won't get lost."

"Thank you." Porterfield shifted his valise and turned up the stairs to the road. He asked directions for the livery stable. Busy men replied in the fewest words necessary, they weren't rude exactly, just not any more helpful than they had to be. "Town must be a haven for Irishmen." Porterfield thought and would have welcomed a measure of them into the ranks. "Make good fighters at your back, in your face they were a terror."

The seat of Taylor County, the town of Grafton was wedged into a valley carved by the River. It was spare and efficient with a newspaper, restaurant, hotel, a business center and the barest necessities for carrying on commerce. Compared to Richmond Grafton was an outpost but Fetterman was the frontier with only a blacksmith's shop, a store, a post office and a log schoolhouse. If troops were waiting for him here they would at least be easy to find.

Porterfield inquired of a woman about where an army might bivouac and she seemed more amused than annoyed. She pointed to the general store. Three or four strangers had been hanging out there, gangly men in strange clothes, she surmised that they might be the army the officer inquired of. True enough. Lounging inside by the stove was indeed the colonel's "army", perhaps six men, chinning with the locals, two Revolutionary-vintage flintlocks eased against the wall.

Red coals of panic glowed down deep in Porterfield's composure. No uniforms, no weapons, no army, and these men carrying on as if they were guests of the county. What was Richmond thinking? Porterfield inquired whether or not there might be other men more serious about their duties camped about.

"Well Pruntytown to the northwest had some fellows who might be persuaded to the Southern cause. And there was the postmaster in charge of the telegraph, he would be of help. About two and a half miles away." The shop keeper turned back to his ledgers, then looked up in a by the way, "Whatever you're thinking about doing you had better be doing it. Ben Kelley is up at Wheeling getting his regiment commissioned. Only a matter of time before he comes through here."

There was more, some good news and bad news. A small company of militia — Barbour Grays was being organized at Philippi. The bad news was that George Latham, lawyer, newspaper publisher and Grafton's intemperate Union conscience was organizing a company or two of Union hot heads to clean out the nest of traitors threatening the area. It might be wise for the commander to put some distance between Latham's temper and his "army" — give it time and space to grow.

Porterfield thanked the shopkeeper for his hospitality

and asked whether the man might have some information about a Major Goff who was supposed to be coming up from Richmond with arms, ammunition and troops. The storekeeper suggested that J.K. Smith, Fetterman's telegraph operator might be of some use in inquiring where the wayward officer might be.

The shopkeeper had been right. At the outset Smith proved most efficient, providing him with lodgings and a base of operations. Messages came and went. The comebacks were not what optimism is fed on. Goff with the cause-saving supplies was still on the other side of Rich Mountain at Beverly, fifty miles to the east and had not set specifics as to his arrival. Porterfield turned to Smith again to send an urgent request to Harpers Ferry for a few pieces of artillery to tide them over should he be attacked. Reply came from Commander Thomas J. Jackson. In spite of Harpers Ferry having been a weapons and ammunition center — the arms works had been set afire when the Yanks evacuated — there was nothing the Confederate Commander could send him. Yes, things were moving right along.

Porterfield established headquarters at Fetterman to be near his one ally the telegraph operator, the only lifeline the colonel had to Richmond. It was there the Confederate waited for the walls to come tumbling down.

With little else to do until his troops arrived or until Richmond responded to his urgent SOS's, Porterfield stared out the window, wondering who would come first over the hills that encircled the little town — Latham or Goff?

Smith had reported that Union governors were turning away volunteers. Ohio, Pennsylvania and New York had men standing by over and above their quotas.

Kelley, he knew by reputation, not to be a patient man. The cause that struck first and decisively would take the counties, the river and the railroad. He had to act, the music that played so agreeable upon a commander's ear, of sergeants barking and men drilling, was mute. So far his army was still only a figment of his imagination. Porterfield needed a miracle.

And there was the X Factor. He pumped his cigar, it helped him think. Lincoln versus Davis. The officer frowned. Lincoln was mocked in the North; vilified in the South, as an incompetent and a baboon. That was something both sides could agree on. But it didn't tally in Porterfield's account book. A man does not come out of the frontier to become a master legal strategist for the Illinois Central Railroad by being slow or lazy. Businessmen don't pay lawyers huge sums if they were stupid, and Lincoln had rarely lost a case. A dark horse does not unseat a party's favorite son the veteran warrior of the Senate Frederick Seward by being easily confounded. And he does not win a national election with secessionist blackmail staring the electorate in the face, by being unpopular. Lincoln and the Republicans had taken the White House. Something more than luck at work here. Porterfield prided himself on sizing up an adversary and Lincoln although an unknown quantity, was a man not to be shortchanged.

And then there was the President of the Confederacy, lately relocating his capital to the more genteel Richmond from Montgomery, Alabama. Jefferson Davis had been West Point educated, baptized in the Mexican War, Secretary of War under Pierce, and served in Congress. But Davis' people had come from Pennsylvania, only two generations in the South. Did he know the South well enough to lead them? Was he one of them? Did he know as much about statecraft as military science? He had not been elected, but chosen for being neither too radical nor too conservative. Would he please all of them or none?

Before he had boarded the train West, Porterfield had conferred with Davis and found him cold and unyielding in his opinions as to what it would take to save the western counties. Porterfield puffed harder on his cigar and pulled at his moustache. Back in Richmond they couldn't possibly understand the political and military terrain here. He hadn't until he had seen it first hand. They were letting him scavenge. The five regiments promised had not arrived. So far he had not even enough for a decent picket. And it was he in this untenable place who would ultimately be held responsible if the whole campaign failed. He didn't want to think of that; the Confederate Congress and the newspapers would roast him alive!

He must move! He would not wait here to be strangled. "Lieutenant!"

A sharp, anxious, well-scrubbed young officer with VMI brass glistening on his uniform coat, entered the rough room. "Yes, Sir."

"Pack up. We're moving to Philippi. Notify the appropriate people as to our whereabouts. We aren't going to just sit here and wait for Latham to knock down our door. It's barely a Sunday walk from Grafton to Philippi but it's a little more distance between Wheeling and there. At least it will put us on the Railroad."

"Yes, Sir."

"And Lieutenant, how is the drill coming?"

"It isn't, Sir." The young officer looked as if his head master had quizzed him on a question for which he had no suitable answer. "I was hoping to train these few men and have them train what troops we get. But they don't feel that drill is necessary...waste of time. They feel they can hunt Yankees pretty much like they hunt everything else around here."

"Lieutenant, an army isn't a flock of geese or a herd of deer to be stalked. There are methods."

"Yes, Sir. But they don't like taking orders. Said they've been stockin' game since before Bosworth and I were born." Lieutenant Gittings sighed. His classmate, John W. Bosworth, had given it his all, but the men were without the proper respect for superior officers especially if they were pups.

"Well, something will have to be done when we get to Philippi."

"Yes, Sir."

Philippi's Virginia House Hotel was far more comfortable for a man of his authority than the back room of a Fetterman store. Porterfield ran up his standard the blue and white Palmetto flag, over the door and moved in. Business picked up. Barbour Grays presented themselves for duty if it were duty of their liking. The Colonel set up a drill camp on the commons in front of the long, covered bridge. If the Grays were game a small troop of Marion Guards would also reluctantly give the process a try.

Porterfield felt more like a commander, at least he had something to command. Word arrived that weapons and supplies were coming from Staunton with a cavalry escort. The trains brought something resembling a uniform, plain hunting shirts, and hats at a cost of $3.00 per man which would later be deducted from a soldier's pay. Porterfield scowled, this would not exactly bring recruits storming to the doors. He put the bill into the drawer.

Porterfield would have been comforted to know that the wagon train was indeed on its way. As it came on, it drew more and more men to it like a magnet: The Highlanders, the Franklin Guards, a troop of Virginia Partisan Rangers led by

John H. McNeill from Pocahontas County. They would have come sooner if they had not been misdirected to another part of the region.

The sharp reports of rapid fire profanity filtered up from one of the young VMI instructors, it was music to the Colonel's ears. Drill. But he made a mental note to talk to the lieutenant, better tone down his enthusiasm. Decent people of Philippi might be offended.

Porterfield struck a match and lit the last of his stock of cigars. Major Boykin stepped inside with another wire. From Jackson at Harpers Ferry, "Hold at all costs. The B & O is worth an army." Jackson is a good man with orders, but so far he had been stingy with everything — men, supplies, weapons — to hold it with.

"Sir? One more thing."

"Major?"

"Rations."

"What about them?"

"We are out...Sir."

"What have we been feeding the men with?"

"The men have been taking to the hills, game mostly, cooking it up on the grounds. But sometimes, they're tired, and so they take the easy way...a chicken...a sheep from a local pasture or pen."

Porterfield swore. The Colonel took the Secretary of War's name in vain quite often of late. It was his sole luxury now that the cigars were about out. Leroy Pope Walker was a bureaucrat, his backside shinny from too much sitting. It did not take a tactical genius to know that Porterfield had to get men with muskets and cannon on those ridges with all possible dispatch. And an army rode on its stomach.

If Kelley gets cannon up on the hills first, there would be hell to pay. Shelling Philippi from up there would be like shooting ducks in a barrel — a few ducks at this point — but a slaughter just the same. Support must come.

Support, of a sorts, was just over the ridge. Captain Stofer and his Pocahontas County Volunteers were taking the long way around a piece of farm equipment. Near Huttonsville the mud-splattered company came upon a McCormack mowing machine. The men gathered around it never having seen the invention before and not sure whether it was friend or foe. One young patriot was not taking any chances. He took estimation of the contraption and shouted, "It's a cannon, I tell ye fellers. That's what it is."

IX

Porterfield had been on the job less than a month and he was feeling more optimistic than a commander should. His numbers were up to slightly better than battalion strength — about one hundred thirty men who knew little more about military drill than their left from their right foot.

Porterfield smiled. It was time to flex some muscle — "blood his troops" — as the term goes. A small offensive action — nothing complex — to see how they stood up to the enemy. A little show of spirit would motivate the men toward some much needed drill and discipline. And the word would be out that the Confederates could sting. Help in recruiting.

And the Colonel had just the objective in mind. The Union colors flying over the Ward Hotel had been an annoyance since the day he had stepped off the train. The Hotel was Latham's Grafton's Headquarters, the county seat for all Unionist activity in the area. The coast was clear, the commander was in Wheeling enrolling his Grafton Guards into the Union Army. Without their fiery leader the town would be easy pickin's.

Jackson had been on him again to take Grafton with whatever troops at hand. "When you march on the place, resolve to take it and after it is in your possession, don't entertain for an instant the idea of giving it up. Success to you."

"Old Blue Light" rode to the sound of the offensive. The Presbyterian deacon was quite something. He had demonstrated not only a taste for war in Mexico but had become a connoisseur of it. Thomas Jackson had graduated from West Point the same year as McClellan but went on to teach Artillery Tactics at the Virginia Military Institute. He had no patience for laggards. At the VMI he drilled his students with his two famous rules for battle: surprise the enemy, and once on him, never let up.

If Porterfield waited too long there would be the devil to pay. He reread Jackson's wire and slipped it in the drawer with the accumulation of official memoranda that was big on advice and light on support. Porterfield smiled. Grafton could just be the first Confederate victory, if he just played his cards right.

"Lieutenant?" Gittings was shocked to see his superior smiling. "Organize the men and send Captain Robinson in here. He's going to Grafton."

A smile broke over the subordinate's face like sunrise. "Yes, Sir." Gittings crossed the office for the Palmetto standard to run up on the victorious ground. "Lieutenant, I feel like a cigar."

"Sorry, Sir."

"Damn that Walker! Can't he even provide for the basic necessities? A Southerner without a cigar — treason!" Biggest damm cigar factory was right up there in Wheeling and Latham is probably puffing away at this moment."

But Porterfield mellowed, probably plenty in his drawer at the Ward Hotel just waiting to be liberated. He hummed the little jingle the children sang as they passed his window on their way to and from school. He came around his desk and nearly upended his subordinate — his aristocratic features frozen in shock. Porterfield recoiled, aware for the first time the little ditty he had been happily humming, "We'll Hang Ole Jeff Davis From a Sour Apple Tree." Porterfield coughed and rubbed his nose, "That will be all, Lieutenant."

The orderly saluted and left.

"Bastard, should hang him from any tree near at hand. Where's my men, my guns, my rations, my artillery, my powder, and my dammed cigars? Hangings too good for him!"

The Letcher Guards, Barbour Lighthorse Cavalry and Harrison's State Guards with Captain John Robinson at their head lined up and were ready to move by afternoon. The men felt good, they were finally getting out of Philippi — the neighbors had been irritable of late. The men were happy to be doing something about the war other than just drilling.

It had stopped raining, the sun was warm, and there were no delays from their Union neighbors. On the way the men picked berries and made a good time of it. They would have felt a little better if everyone were armed, but still they would make an impression.

At the west edge of Grafton's Main Street word passed among the citizens without fuss that the town was having company. Robinson ordered the troops to proceed down the middle of town toward Latham's office at the Ward Hotel. The troops closed up but maintained common pace through a gauntlet of curses, jeers, and epithets of inhospitable welcome. Someone had found an expanse of bunting and stretched it across the road to block the cavalry. One of the dragoons charged his horse forward to jump the barrier. The horse's back hoof caught in the folds, pulling the banner down.

Robinson smiled, "One flag down and one to go." He urged his men on. Ahead Latham's office and recruiting station. The commander reined up in front of the hotel the citizenry gathering to see what happened next. Robinson eased back in the saddle and surveyed the scene. The townspeople were unarmed as well, Robinson relaxed.

Pointing to the Union flag mounted in an upper story, he gave the order. "Go up there and tear that damned rag down." Two privates turned for the porch with a howl. Only a single hotel employee stood in their way. Before he could be brushed aside, the man picked up a chair from the porch and hurled it at the commander, knocking him from his horse into the muddy street.

His men helped the captain to his feet. His face flushed with rage, Robinson raised his arm to order a second charge at the hotel. Before he could follow through, the twilight cracked with the thunder of musket hammers drawn back and cocked. The Confederates looked up. Silhouetted against the horizon were Latham's Guards balanced on the rooftops, stretching out of windows and doorways, leaning over fences, taking aim on the force in the street.

Fate wavered between two beats of the heart. Robinson's arm froze at half mast. Townsmen moved back. The flag billowed in the wind. The Captain watched it ripple. Slowly he shook his head. Not today and not over this. He ordered his men to stand at ease. The Union militia lowered their weapons.

Granted safe retreat, Robinson turned to his aide, "Order the men to withdraw, Lieutenant." First blood would not be drawn here.

X

Private Thornbury Bailey Brown and a friend Second Lieutenant Daniel Wilson of the victorious Latham Guards, were feeling good about their day's work with the Confederates. A moral victory of sorts. Filled with Union spirit and probably some of the more liquid variety, they had taken the long way to Pruntytown around Fetterman and the Confederate pickets to catch the train at Valley Falls for Wheeling, and to join up. They decided to bypass the long bridge. A sufficient Confederate Camp was stationed there to be inconvenient if not dangerous and they decided instead on the long road into town. No use tempting fate.

They were veterans now; had seen the elephant, so to speak. There was plenty of time before the train and they stopped at a tavern in Pruntytown for a little fortification. The reception was fit for conquering heroes. Unionists toasted the boys. One toast led to another and with the accumulation of toasts Bailey Brown's war spirit got the best of him. He raised a glass and dared, "Before the night is over I will have some Rebel blood, or go to hell!"

More glasses were raised and more alcohol consumed, the last train for Wheeling had long past. The hour late, the two heroes pressed the shortest route home which passed the Confederate pickets at the long bridge. It was the same route they had been so careful to avoid that afternoon. Still exuberant and thoroughly sauced, Brown and Wilson made unsteady headway until Confederate pickets ordered them to stop. They were local boys Daniel Knight, George Glenn and William Reese who stepped out of the shelter of the Long Bridge and repeated the order for their two neighbors to halt and identify themselves. It was only a formality because Knight and Brown were well known to each other as mutual antagonists long before secession separated them politically. Brown wavered. He called for Knight to step out where he could see him better. "That you, Knight?"

"Private Daniel Knight, of the Letcher Guards. Step forward and be recognized."

Brown slapped Wilson on the shoulder. "That ain't a Confederate." Brown peered into the darkness, "It's a chicken thief. You ain't got the breeding of a skunk or the brains of a buzzard to be a real soldier. This man shot my cow. That's the only thing he can hit. Come on, Wilson. I got to pee. Mind, he may bash you by accident with that cannon." And the boys moved on.

"You stay right there and don't move till we call the captain." Knight raised his musket.

"If you insist." Brown stood still and things were at a stalemate until Knight felt warm spray against his shin. "You son of a...I'm takin' you to the captain!" Knight shook with anger.

"You ain't takin' me nowhere." Brown drew a pistol from his belt and pulled the trigger. A shot buzzed by Knight's ear. Knight clasped the musket to his cheek, pulled the trigger and the pan flashed. The ball exploded out of the barrel striking Brown in the chest. He dropped to his knees. Wilson pulled his friend to his feet, and hoped to be off before the sentry could reload. Brown tried to stand, "I think I can make it." And he collapsed dead.

"I think you are dead." Wilson hovered over his friend but not for long. Glenn got off a shot that struck Wilson in the foot. Wounded and bleeding, Wilson abandoned his friend and escaped into the darkness. He hobbled to Grafton to spread the alarm. In quick course, Wheeling papers gave the news that the war had claimed its first Union casualty.

XI

The fuse was burning down to the powder keg; war to be ignited not by a martyr but by a blood feud. How little control presidents and commanders really have in these matters. The Yankees will be coming now.

Private Daniel Knight, stood dishevelled and puffy-eyed in Porterfield's office. None of them had slept. The sentry had answered question for question until the Colonel was dry. It had gone on for hours. In turn, the boy had been indignant, defiant, arrogant, but not repentent. The commander wished he could put the boy in front of a firing squad just for insubordination, or at least have him flogged. Porterfield sighed, the British had all the fun.

"Do you know what you have done?" The Colonel was losing patience.

"Killed me a Yankee." Knight answered evenly.

"You may have started a war."

"If the Yankees want to go to war over one drunken rebel, I guess that's their business. As I see it, war is going to happen one way or the other, might as well be here where we can squash it."

The Commander kept his hands clenched behind his back. He had half a notion to...but it would accomplish nothing. He picked up Lieutenant Kimble's reports. VMI produced astonishing alumni. Say what you did about Jackson, his students were first rate. Kimble had uncovered a lot in a few hours.

Knight was not exactly a saint, he had been accused of stealing a beehive and slashed the arresting officer with a knife. Later there were charges of shooting a neighbor's cow. Knight had been sitting on his porch, gun in his lap when Bailey Brown and the sheriff came up to arrest him. Brown charged him, took the gun and there had been some violent words. Porterfield sighed.   Is this the stuff on which Richmond wanted him to build an army?

"Lieutenant?" Gittings returned after turning Knight over to the guard. "Latham has taken his militia to Wheeling. Isn't that what our sources tell us?"

"Yes, Sir. First West Virginia Volunteers."

"Thank you, Lieutenant. Well, let's get out of here before they make us their first priority and stuff us up in this crevice like a fish down a bottle and cork it behind us. Grafton has rations there and room to move. You know what to do."

The Colonel sighed. Another change of base. Porterfield's star was not rising. In Richmond, Lee was not pleased with his progress, recruiting was well-below anticipated levels to meet escalating events. Although a couple of volunteer companies full of bluster and threats trickled in they were undisciplined, ill-equipped, and unready. They were fired up to fight Yankees, but were quarrelsome about the necessity of drill. And it had begun to rain — the blasted rain. If the wagons and troops were coming over the mountains, the rain would not just slow them down but bottomless ruts and gullies of mud would glue them down to a full stop.

What ammunition pickets had, they kept in their pockets where it got damp from rain or perspiration and would not shoot. But then few had anything to shoot with — not enough guns to even keep the pickets armed.

Would the Yankees with arsenals and warehouses full of Enfields and Springfields, cartridge boxes to a man, be so hospitable as to attack on a hot sunny day when our powder was dry?

Porterfield sat down to his desk, pulled out

stationery, and started to write orders that sent Captain Christian Roberts and his Virginia Militia to fire the railroad bridge connecting Wheeling and Marietta. He was then to take similar measures to other bridges and tunnels, in order to secure their new headquarters at Grafton. If this couldn't stop the Yankees, it would at least slow them down.

The Commander then dispatched four more companies of cavalry including James Wiley on other bridge-burning missions. Porterfield folded the papers and gave them to his aides to dispatch after headquarters had been effectively moved.

The orders were filled with an enthusiasm. The arteries were severed. One cavalry detail was so motivated that they were on the wrong side of the bridge when they set it afire. They had to walk thirty-five miles back to Grafton by another route.

Like it or not Grafton was going to be home, and the local citizens did not like it. The Irish, never people to acquiesce to invaders, had been proficient in showing their inhospitality although there had been no violence yet. The untrained Quartermaster was finding it hard to feed the men and provide forage for the horses. Locals were not being generous and forcible confiscation could provoke another mishap. Drill was not progressing on schedule. Porterfield could be forgiven if he were contemplating another line of work.

From his office in the state capitol in Columbus General George McClellan regarded the bridge burning acts of rebellion. Jacob Cox at Camp Dennison was ordered to organize troops and have them ready to move. The camp teemed with regiments in various stages of training and Cox readied the most advanced — the Virginia Volunteers and the 14th and 18th Ohio Volunteers — and hustled them on to a train. Two more regiments from Indiana were put on alert.

Smith was at the telegraph key to take down McClellan's instructions and he handed them to one of Porterfield's couriers. The Yankees were coming.

"Lieutenant?"

Gittings slammed through the door, "Lieutenant get the fastest horse you can. You are going to Richmond." Porterfield drafted another appeal to President Davis and his military advisor, Robert E. Lee briefing them of the alarming situation and his paramount need for support.

The Commander was not satisfied with the reply. He clenched the manifest in his hand and attacked his young Lieutenant with unbridled anger. A few army pistols, some double- and single-barreled shotguns and enough sabers to arm the men was all Richmond sent. There was a wagon load of about five hundred shirts and one hundred pairs of pants to be issued over the signatures of the captains who would later be responsible for payment. The President asked the Colonel to appreciate his position. The individual states were responsible for arming and clothing their own regiments, it was impossible for Richmond to make a special case out of western Virginia. Porterfield must make due with what they sent.

The Colonel exploded, "Lieutenant, did our esteemed Secretary of War perhaps include a suggestion as to exactly how my men armed with sabers like a bunch of pirates were going to hold off the Yankees and their rifles and cannon? Why didn't they just send us pikes, bows and arrows?"

"Sir, I think Colonel Jackson has made arrangements for just that — arming men with pikes, I mean."

"It was a rhetorical question, Lieutenant."

"Yes, Sir." Gittings held no ill feeling. For weeks he had watched his commander deteriorate from a swaggering officer into a hollow-eyed, bare-bones insomniac.

"I'm sorry, Lieutenant. Get yourself some dinner. Well done."

Gittings did not move, "Sir?" He reached inside his tunic and pulled out a small box.

Porterfield took it. Cigars! The Commander was deeply touched. "Thank you, Lieutenant." He opened the box gently and presented one to his aide. Then took one himself, bit off the end and put it into his mouth. As Gittings lit his cigar Porterfield puffed as if life-saving oxygen were rolled inside with the tobacco. The office filled with gray smoke and the commander inhaled it euphorically.

McClellan was coming from Cincinnati with at least two armed regiments, and a battery, possibly more. Kelley was in Wheeling with about one thousand more men including Latham's blasted vigilantes. There was another regiment moving this way from Marietta under that transplanted American lawyer Jacob Cox. And heaven knows who else was coming! For all he knew every mother's son north of the Ohio was pulling on Union blue and taking up a rifle and forwarding his mail to Grafton.

He, on the other hand, was going to make a stand with no trained troops, no guns, no cannon. He had farm boys armed with cheese knives. But at that instant Porterfield was a contented man. The Yankees could have swarmed down upon him, and the Colonel would not have fired a shot — not for a second would he spoil this moment.

While burning a bridge Captain Roberts met with Union resistance and was killed, but his men went on to finish the bridge over Simpson's Creek. Colonel Jackson at Harpers Ferry who had been hot to burn the bridges in the first place had been replaced by Joseph Johnston. Still no reinforcements from that direction. Lee also sent Porterfield his regrets. Since events were heating up at Richmond's front and back doors he could not spare a man, but he could send about one thousand muskets and powder. The wire operator Smith kept Porterfield informed that McClellan had given Kelley the go ahead to put an end to the bridge burning.

If a commander cannot keep ahead of events, events over run him. Porterfield, his small army surrounded by unfriendly Union citizens, moved back to Philippi and made plans to fall back to Beverly if necessary. News from the telegraph office was that Federals were in Fairmont on the B & O twenty miles to the northwest. Bridgeburner Wiley had been unable to destroy the railroad over the Cheat River or blow up the tunnel at Rowlesburg, that left the back door open to attack.

It had been not quite a month since Porterfield had stepped off that train in Grafton. Grafton, Fetterman, and Pruntytown had proved unlucky for Confederate fortunes, Philippi was turning out no better.

Porterfield had about fourteen companies — nine hundred men including the Upshur County Grays just in — and a company of Rockbridge County Cavalry. Porterfield took his case to the people trying to rally them around the defense of mother Virginia. The citizens saw things differently.

Porterfield was being surrounded. McClellan had sent his aide Colonel Frederick Lander, who was beyond the age of most generals, yet a talented, robust, profane and God fearing commander, to lend a hand. Colonel Kelley was now in Grafton, the 14th Ohio was in Clarksburg twenty miles to the northwest. A third detachment of Indiana militia under Brigadier-General Thomas Morris arrived. As ranking officer he took command and planned an attack.

Morris gave the order for Kelley and Lander to march

to Philippi in two parallel columns on either side of the Tygart River. If Porterfield is listening in on the wires, (and by now they were sure he was), he would hear instructions for Kelley to move against Harpers Ferry. Instead the Irishman was to move south keeping to the Moatsville Road and position himself above Philippi to the east and be ready to attack at first light — 4:00 a.m. on June 3rd. Lander would send Colonel Ebenezer Dumont and nearly 1,500 men, accompanied by artillery, down the Beverly-Fairmont Pike along the western side of the River. Dumont was to arrive at the same time, about four o'clock, and wait for Kelley's signal. When all was in place Kelley would fire his pistol and both sides would converge upon the town — shutting both front and back doors.

It is impossible to move nearly three thousand men through mountainous, forested country without attracting some attention. Porterfield received various reports that the Yankees were on the move. He readied his men to evacuate — that unpleasantness at Grafton had given him all the taste of a duck shoot he wanted. All day June 2nd, wagons were loaded and the troops were ready to move. Then it began to rain.

To protect precious supplies from spoilage, wagons were unloaded and their contents stored in barns. The rain pounded harder and men ran for cover. Roads would be a quagmire. Porterfield cut orders to delay the evacuation until morning. Cavalry was sent out in reconnaissance. Instead of riding circuit around the town they returned about midnight in the slashing rain. Pickets, who would have been on guard on the roads and by ways in more agreeable weather, were sleeping dry and warm under barn roofs in Philippi. A Confederate Captain stood back from the window at the Barbour House and shook his head, "Hell, any army marching to-night must be made up of a set of damned fools!"

Fools or not the Yankees were coming on. In columns of fours, heads bent against the rain, marching through the black void without the usual ten minute rests every hour. Kelley was not about to let his men straggle and his cannon sink down in the mud. So he kept them at it. Men chewed coffee and hardtack on the march. Officers herded them along.

In plenty of time Dumont's forces took up their assigned positions above the river. But Kelley was late having taken a wrong turn in the inky blackness. Dumont had word that Kelley's advance was just coming down the road and would be in position soon. Dumont leaned back in his saddle and waited.

Soldiers trooping past the house awakened Mrs. Humphreys. She looked out. It had stopped raining. The soldiers were passing in good order in spite of the mud. Her first thoughts were for her son among the Philippi defenders. It did not take a tactical genius to realize that Philippi must be warned that Yankees were upon them. Mrs. Humphreys dressed hurridly and roused her nine-year-old son Oliver. With instructions ringing in his ears, she pushed him up on a horse and led it out to the road. Blue troops moved around them, but a young officer was not about to have the boy alert the Confederates and pulled him down from his mount.

In a rage Mrs. Humphreys started pelting the ill-mannered Yankees with sticks, rocks and whatever missiles within her grasp. The Yankees summoned what courtesy they had, considering their wet, tired, foot-sore, hungry state, and tried to subdue the woman. But Mrs. Humphreys was nothing if not persistent. She hustled her son back on the horse in defiance. The officer pulled him down again. Her

Christian patience exasperated, the woman pulled a pistol from inside the bodice of her dress and fired point blank at the officer. Miraculously she missed. The soldiers drew arms, but the officer waved them down. Before they could be arrested or worse, mother and son retreated into the house.

The report of the pistol shot echoed along the perimeter of hills. Colonel Dumont waiting above the massive two-lane, shad bridge at the mouth of Philippi road smiled. He had his signal. He turned to his officers to give the order to attack.

The woman had accomplished her mission beyond her wildest comprehension. Dumont had his signal but Kelley was not yet up. Events took control. Two, six-pound cannon rang fire down on the city from the heights. The barrage was a wake-up call for the sleepy Confederates. Some soldiers were still sleeping in, others were lazily dressing. Outside the earliest risers were boiling up the first cups of coffee to clear the fog from their brains and warm the muscles cramped with camp lumbago.

Union Colonel Robert Milroy, who had also been wandering the hills of western Virginia thanks to the misdirection of his guide, heard the signal. He was not a man to be caught tardy. He ordered his 9th Indiana troops down the hill behind the Court House ready for they did not know yet what, but they would not be late when it came.

Dumont's Indiana troops stormed the shad bridge and crossed it, clearing out the Confederate pickets. Once on the other side, they lined up in formation on either side of the road and waited. Kelley and his western Virginians would have the honor of being first into town.

Kelley heard the shot and knew he was late. Not one to miss a grand entrance, he called for the double quick. He reined his horse down the road, rallying his troops through the bridge between Dumont's guard of honor. There was no time to secure the back road out of town. They rushed to the agreed-upon rendezvous. With courtesies met, Dumont reined his horse down Talbot Hill at break-neck speed heading toward the bridge to drive his men on.

Kelley's troops met the first Confederates drawing up in line. One of the Confederates drew a bead on the Union officer riding hell bent for leather down upon them. He got him in his sights and pulled the trigger. Kelley clutched his chest, blood oozing between the fingers of his gauntlets.

A second line of defenders were drawing up in an orchard behind the schoolhouse. Kelley struggled to remain in the saddle but fell into the road. Thinking their leader dead, his men spurred on with fiery vengence, storming the Confederate resistence with a rage.

Blood gushed from their commanders wounds as his aides carried him to a nearby porch. Mrs. Barron, wife of the owner of the Barbour House fetched a blanket and had him moved into the front room where the Colonel would be more comfortable. She put a towel to the wound on his right breast. The colonel gasped. Breath came with stabs of pain and wheezes. The bullet had pierced a lung. She looked up at the anxious men of the 7th. "It's mortal. He will die." But Kelley did not die.

News of the casualty spread through the forces like a fever. Confederate resistance was broken and untrained men turned for the rear of town. A squad of Kelley's troops mounted the Virginia House headquarters, an officer slit the ropes and the blue Palmetto flag drifted down into the mud. Not to be without their own souvenir, Company E of Kelley's 7th Indiana pulled down the Stars and Bars from the courthouse pole and ran up the Stars and Stripes. Cavalry guidons — swallow-tail penants — were taken and also an elegant, green, silk banner with golden fringe and bullions which had been abandoned in a supply wagon in the panic. All of the supplies Porterfield had painfully gathered were captured.

Milroy's 9th Indiana chased Confederates through the forested hills, while Kelley's men pursued others down the Beverly Pike. With no force posted at the back door the Confederates made a run for the hills.

The thunder of the first cannon rang like bells of doom. Porterfield closed his eyes. "The Yankees!" The Commander strapped on his sword and flew out the door to rally his Confederates. They filtered around him as if he were no more of an inconvenience than a stick in the middle of a swiftly-moving river. He pulled at one and motioned him to form a line. Wild-eyed the soldier pulled away and bolted for the rear.

Porterfield knew even a small organized advance could have stopped the Federals at the front door, bottled them up at the covered bridge to give him time to form a second line further back. But defense was not on the minds of the troops who would have been gone had it not rained the night before. Now they were making up for lost time.

Behind them lay Laurel and Rich Mountains and the Confederates rushed to it. George Latham smiled, the sulphur and powder black on his face. "Run, you sons of a ..."

Philippi lit the fuse of the Civil War and Nolan Giles had his wish. There was enemy and a war waiting for him compliments of Colonel George Porterfield, CSA. And for any soldier — Blue or Gray — there would be plenty of war to go around.

XII

"It's a forage cap, Boy! It goes on your head like this," Sergeant Chase jerked the hat down but it bobbed up on Nolan's blonde waves like a blue duck. Military specifications — one size fits all — seemed to be of some debate here. Caps balanced on some crowns like a coffee cup while other soldiers were thankful for a wide set of ears that kept theirs from falling over their faces like a hangman's sack.

"Damned contractors. You!" Chase switched headgear with a passing recruit to their mutual satisfaction. The Sergeant placed it on the boy's crown and snapped the leather straps snug across the front.

The Fourth had been issued uniforms in stages; the pants, then the coats and now the caps. Men who knew nothing about sewing but knew a lot about craftsmanship, realized that government issue was of shabby quality. It spoiled the morale. Chase was annoyed. It was a graduation of sorts and the men had turned out choice. They deserved better.

The Sergeant-Major surveyed his brood proudly and caught himself smiling. Must watch himself, no good letting them see that. The Company — the regiment as a whole — had shaped up smartly to be among the finest in camp. Companies C and F marched to the left and right flank of the regiment. As skirmishers they had been awarded the .58 caliber, rifled Enfields. The rest of the regiment were issued buck and ball and the .69 caliber smoothbores.

The four comrades in arms would make good point men. Mr. Giles over there will be okay as long as he listens to his Hibernian guardian angel. But there was only so much discipline you could expect from that one. He had something else though — the fires of a good sergeant — maybe even a regular. Heaven help us!

Quinn had the deliberation and control of an officer. A curious one him. In the old country they would be enemies, here they were on the same side. There were a lot of them Emerald Irish filling the ranks sure enough. Quinn better than most.

Mac was Scot through and through — frugal, looking after his mates. Chase frowned, something delicate about the lad though. Already he was racked with the camp cough. It had started among all the boys because of the wet spring. As regular as reveille, the morning ritual of clearing the ague and night vapors out of your chest began. Soon the whole camp was coughing to a man — like a pack of barking dogs.

Christie. Chase frowned. A curious case him. One of those set upon the earth alone — no family except for a mother who never wrote. No other attachments for such a brotherly man; no religion or traditions — nothing to keep him strung together during the hard times. There was a darkness about him, behind that Irish smile that flashed when he was happy and when he was the opposite. Bore watching...that one.

Dennison was a cut above the lot of training camps. Pushed harder, demanded better, and now the governor had decided against the futility of sending ninety-day enlistments into the field — wise move. Just as the men would be getting into the field, maybe even getting a battle under their belts, they would be going home. Likely as not re-enlist. Instead McClellan decided to send only three-year men. Made sense.

This was not a peacock army like the pictures he had seen of Napoleon or Wellington, soldiers decked out in white breeches, leggings, glistening black knee boots, tunics iridescent with brass and braid, gaudy shakos. This was an army of farmers, shop keepers, and mechanics, volunteers all of them led by no-nonsense commanders, for the most part equally nondescript. Their only glitter were rows of brass buttons and gold-embroidered shoulder straps. Maybe a silk sash, otherwise they had forsaken the plumage, medals, and other geegaws because such folderol was hard to keep up in the field. There was a business about these men of Puritan purpose, of Calvinistic efficiency and equality, rather than glory and empire.

The best lot yet, Chase eyed them as choice, so much so that he had called in his markers and requested a transfer. He opted to be attached to Colonel Andrews' headquarters. Cox had tried to keep him--a valuable man with trains unloading civilians by the hour. But the Sergeant-Major protested. He was becoming too old to wet-nurse another regiment. A man needed some battle to keep his talents sharp. Chase padded the flask nestled under his tunic. Yes, he had a right to celebrate. Now to see to the lads.

Nolan shoved four inches of Saxon-blue wool down into his socks. Stood up and his pants bloomed around his legs like Zouave pantaloons. "Good boy," Chase nodded. "Keep the peskies and dust from stinging your legs on the march." The square-toed, black Brogans stretched out like a couple of coal barges. The four buttons of the dark blue wool coat barely met over his stomach. "The first hundred miles of the march will trim your ballast, Boy, and the coat will fit tailor made."

But the mystery at hand was the forage cap — a hang-dog version of the officer's kepi. Men balanced the long, flat crown forward and back. The eight-inch tall, cylinder of blue wool looked like a pancake balanced on top of the recruit's head. The thin slice of leather brim was not wide enough to shield the eyes from a blasting sun, nor the rain either.

"I don't know, Sergeant. What's it good for?" Quinn challenged the man who seemed an inexhaustible source of military history, protocol, and tactics. They had almost tired of stumping their Sergeant, but Quinn still rose to the dare when he smelled the opportunity.

"It's tradition. It's good for your horse if your asking." Chase pulled off his own worn cap. A shock of white scar streaked like lightening from the crown to just behind the left ear, black hair laid to each side. Nolan shivered. So, it had been true what they said about the Indians.

The veteran turned the hat gently over in his hands fairly caressing it, then holding it upside down by the brim. "It's got a history, Mick. What's it look like, Boy?"

Nolan could find nothing in experience to compare it to but Quinn sized it up immediately, "Like a bucket."

"Exactly, Mick. That's what it is, a feed bucket. The French Legionnaire used to feed his horse with his hat which looked much like this one — only stiff and white to fight back the sun. Ours is blue...just the opposite...going to fry your head like a bean but that's Army wisdom for you.

"However, a trooper is responsible for the most important equipment he has — his mount and his hat is the feed bucket. He just scooped up the oats in his hat and pulled it up over the horse's nose. Ain't it dandy?"

"Let's give them to the troopers and get a white hat with a brim as big as an umbrella." Nolan summed up the logic.

With buttons trimmed down, shoes blacked the Regiment presented itself for grand review. Then Nolan and Quinn presented themselves front and center at the photogaleria for mementos. One for each of them and one to send to Kathleen. They braced for the lens, solemn as preachers, fully aware of their necessity as national saviors,

82

certainly to be on first name basis with President Lincoln himself. It was only a matter of hours before the President would hear of their reputation and call them into Washington as his personal honor guard.

Jacob Cox, commander of Camp Dennison, said nearly as much when he and General Robert Anderson, the hero of Fort Sumter, mounted the stand at the three-year re-enlistment rally. General Anderson, the Army's poster boy if it had one, had an office in Cincinnati making it convenient for regular visits to Camp Dennison to convert the ninety-day volunteers to three-year regiments.

The General's praise floated over the regiment like perfume and a good time was had by all except for the two ex-residents of Dublin. One sported a purple mouse under his left eye and the other a split lip. While the General painted gallant pictures of chivalry, brotherhood and comrades in arms...

"I guess he don't know that Irish and the Hessians over there in the Ninth take exception to the rule." Chase hissed. Quinn winced, the pain seared across his jaw like lightening. In the Army barely two months, and he had been a casualty in two battles, and he had not even seen the enemy yet.

Camp Dennison had become something of a Babel with Irish, Polish and German recruits--some speaking good English, some enough to get by, and the rest none at all except when it suited them. Otherwise they chose other methods to put their general impressions across.

The Ninth Ohio fell into the last. Commanded by a McCook — of which Ohio was blessed with a profusion, this one a lawyer by the name of Robert L. The Ninth Ohio had arrived at Dennison a couple of weeks after the Fourth had settled in. But the Germans did not respect seniority, and they bowed to no law except their own and their colonel's. He, they followed with a passion. One thousand Germans who spoke no English presented some inconveniences in the way of instruction and discipline. The Deutchmen got their drill and training through an interpreter. The rest was handled as the need arose.

One difference of opinion was that of cuisine. Upon being commissioned a U.S. Regiment, the troops became the responsiblity of the Quartermaster who presented what the Commissary could obtain in food and clothing purchased in large quantities and at low bids. In matters of mess the Germans pushed the plates aside, "Nein!" and saw to other arrangements. The Army had been benevolent to arm them with a reasonably accurate fire arm and provide them with ammunition. The surrounding Hamilton County Forests teamed with game and the Little Miami River had good fishing. So working from the philosphy that God helps those who help themselves, they turned to the Creator's bounty rather than the Army's. When time was short the Germans took a short cut and availed themselves of a duck, hen, or goose from a neighboring farm.

McCook became a familiar figure at headquarters, suffering furious upbraidings that aroused the nearby regiments but to no apparent improvement in his men's behavior.

So when the guard — Nolan and Quinn at this rotation — called a halt to two Germans leaving the grounds without passes the discussion became quite demonstrative. "No pass, no pass" was as simple as Nolan could make it. He raised his Enfield and prayed that the lieutenant would be coming up to attend to matters before they went any further.

Having wasted enough time on meaningless discussion, these being smaller and less intimidating than the usual pickets, the larger German by the name of Tag pushed the smaller inconvenience out of the way. Quinn crossed his musket against his chest and stepped in front of the other German and ordered him to halt. The Niner muttered something about "donnerwetter" that Nolan did not understand. The German pushed the smaller boy to a side and passed. Nolan blocked his path. The German growled but Nolan didn't flinch. The German shoved, Nolan shoved back. A left fist fired a direct hit in the same eye that only just healed after the misunderstanding back on Sandusky Street.

Before Quinn could defend their honor, he intercepted a similar bolt in the right jaw. He went down but not without butting his adversary in the groin with his rifle. The proceedings got underway.

Years of pushing a plow, swinging an ax and digging up boulders had made the prairie boys competitive. The smaller guard tore in like a mad dog — making up in fury and swiftness what he lacked in size and strength. Company C was making a respectable representation of itself when Chase strode up.

Fifteen years fighting Indians had taught the veteran that a knot of men was always a bad sign. This one was growing quickly — an eternity when a man is getting the stuffings beat out of him. By the time Chase waded into the center there were a half dozen Irish engaged in a matter of honor with Germans who had been multiplying in equal proportion. The lot were going at it bare knuckle with a circle of supporters coaching from a safe perimeter.

About the same time Colonel McCook pushed through like a nanny collecting his bluebloods. In defference to his commander, Tag stood back, spitting mud and grass and taking inventory of his molars. Size had been to the advantage of the Germans, except for the mud they came off better. "Sergeant, you need to teach your men a little discipline!" The tenderfoot Colonel barked at the veteran Sergeant-Major.

"Sir." Chase braced accepting the dressing down as a Sergeant must but not liking it.

"Can anyone tell me what is going on?" Irish and Germans alike surveyed the Colonel with something akin to amazement that he did not know what a brawl looked like. Or was this one of those rhetorical questions that lawyers were so fond of? But no one said a word. There was the smell of extra drill and policing for both sides if some suitable explanation wasn't contrived.

"Well?" Sergeant Chase put himself squarely in front of Nolan, as if there were no question as to the source of the trouble. Nolan shrugged. Quinn wiped the blood carefully not to stain his new uniform. They got two a year, anymore and he would have to pay for it himself. "It was nothing, Sergeant, we were just helping the gentlemen."

"Excuse me, Private?" the Colonel boomed.

Quinn weaved in the wind like tender wheat, his Sergeant keeping him perpendicular only as long as he held him aloft by the scruff of his coat. All the pugilists stared gapjawed at the little Irishman as he spit blood out of his mouth, "Yes sir, these gentleman and us — we were discussing the postponement of their safari until such time as they could detail the legal matters when one just stepped off and fell...Sir."

McCook looked bug-eyed at the man's nerve, "He fell down, Private?"

"Something like that, Sir, yes." Quinn could feel the heat of Chase's rage radiate even from arm's length. He did not look that way.

McCook looked at his Germans who understood nothing about the gift of the Blarney Stone, but sensed that a stay of execution might be in the air. They nodded, "Ja!" encouraging it for all they were worth. "Ya, Herr Oberst. Ja, Gefallen."

McCook stared incredulous at the muddy, ragged soldiers and burst into thunderous laughter that rang through the camp. "Ja! In a pig's..."

Sergeant Chase stepped in. "With due respect, I would let it be, Sir."

The lawyer allowed that a case that could be settled out of court was enough due process. Anything more would necessitate reports and more upbraidings "Yes, Sergeant. I understand. Let's see that it doesn't happen again. You take your Irish and I'll take my Germans and perhaps we can save our energies for the Rebels."

As McCook herded his Teutonic Knights back to camp, the German Tag gave Quinn a cocked salute, "Tag und danke." Then followed his colonel.

Co. C 4th OVI
Camp Dennison
1 June 1861

Myra,

Received your last letter. The muffins and the cake were deemed a great service to the country by all those who partook. You are blessed among men here especially since we have been restricted to bread and water for a recent unpleasantness with another regiment. This is a dubious blessing in that we are spared the bad beef. The last portion was saluted and buried with full military honors begetting a Revolutionary War veteran — even if it was a horse.

Troops arrive every day taking up more room. We march only in fine weather, police and guard the rest of the time. But life is mostly full of rain and mud — I despair of ever seeing the sun.

General Cox and Colonel Andrews paid us a visit. I can bet you a month's pay that the cook did not feed them green beef. They raised a general fervor for re-enlisting for three years. The Fourth enlisted nearly to a man.

Last Wednesday, we were paraded in our blue uniforms that seem to melt off our bodies from sheer sunlight. The shoes gap and the soles smile up at us with every step. Sergeant Chase says it's the government contractors — that they should be hanged.

You will be happy to know that we are getting some fine preaching here. Every preacher worth his Bible has taken his turn at us. Even Reverend Harris, who is up for promotion to bishop, went at us at services today attended by the whole regiment. Since they are mandatory even Nolan has been regular. What he hears is another matter.

We have made some fine friends of the Germans over

at the Ninth who are most considerate and noble hosts.

Troops are already on their way to Western Virginia. Hope we are following soon or we will all drowned in the mud.

I think of you here and the thoughts are a comfort. I pray that when this is over peace will reign in every heart and our union will be the next to be recognized.

Quinn

XIII

"They certainly saved the best fare until after we reenlisted. This beef is as dry and sharp as a sliver of pine." Christie sloshed some scalding coffee inside his cheeks to soften it up.

"Don't make sense in the pocketbook. The Army plying us with a bonus and furlough with free transportation home. Mighty generous, only to feed us bone."

"These potatoes need salt and a pat of butter." Christie scooped the stew up in a wad of hard bread. "You can find more things to worry about, Quinn. All you got to worry about is one week of fine living at my Uncle Merton's over in Covington. My Aunt Maude can make a cornbread stuffing that would even make this chicken respectable."

Nolan cleaned his plate into the fire and stood up. "I ain't eating this. Let's go over and see what the Deutch are having for dinner. Nolan disappeared into the wall-tent and came out with the remains of Quinn's gift from Myra.

"Where you going with my cake?"

Nolan seemed undisturbed, "Be impolite to go to dinner without branging a dessert. You comin'?"

Next day the four friends were cinching up their meager possessions into blankets when the bugle wailed assembly. Nolan heard it first and smiled, "Deliverance." Sweet music hailing seven days liberation from mud, rain, leaky tents, army beef, and a purgatory presided over by a cranky Sergeant-Major.

Colonel Lorin Andrews began his remarks before the regiment with an apology. Bad sign. The long and short of it was that Secech were storming up through Western Virginia. There had been a battle at Philippi with more to come maybe as far west as Kentucky and even Cincinnati. Although

General McClellan had things well in hand, there would be no passes issued to cross the river. Christie stifled a profanity.

The company was dismissed and the four friends crawled into their tent to form a new plan. They lay on their backs staring up at the canvas saying nothing, their furlough ticking away. The roof began to pop, rain again. Another profanity.

MacGowan rose on an elbow to face the group, "You know, I ain't got an Aunt Maude, but I've got an Uncle Willis, a black sheep, but a good sort. Met him a couple of times at reunions and always thought he would be an adventure if only I could get away from my mother. Full of the bad seed she warned, you know the kind."

Christie was hopeful, "Speak up."

"He's got a farm about six miles on the otherside of the Little Miami in Loveland, walkable to be sure. Food won't be fancy but it will be plentiful. Good hunter."

"Can I get a bath?" Quinn squirmed, he was sure a bug of some primal origins was creeping down his collar.

"Guess so," Mac was sure that Uncle Willis had never concerned himself about such luxuries but figured something could be arranged. And Mac did want Quinn along, Nolan acquits himself well under his gentle authority.

"Think he would like company?" Nolan felt a need especially for Quinn. He had wanted him to take the free ticket and go back to Dublin. But his "pard" refused, they had argued again about it that morning.

"Expect so. Lives all alone in a cabin in the woods. Sort of a noble savage..."

"Wonder if he is related to Sergeant-Major S. Michael Chase."

Mac ignored Christie's interruption, "Can carry on like the unredeemed if we want — cards, hunt, or just gather dust. Uncle Willis don't keep no schedule or no Bible."

Uncle Willis won by acclimation. But if the vote had been retaken as they stood outside the cabin, it might have been different. The bark scaled off the logs like tufts of fur, black slits of glass squinting at them. The architecture was of the general style but a little larger than an outhouse, a center door, a window on either side, and a wood daub chimney that puffed smoke. There was no porch, only a rough-hewn log for a step and the forest came up to the door. The four stood just beyond the first line of trees and regarded the accommodations.

"I was inside only once as a kid, my mother wouldn't let us stay long...afraid some wild thing might come out from under the bed or I might catch something. At the time it had a sense of pioneer excitement to it."

Nolan never thought he would ever meet the accommodations that would make old Camp Dennison look good, but this came close. "My allegiances are with your mother." It was a debate whether the cabin protected the within from the without or vice versa. He wouldn't bet on it either way.

Christie squared his shoulders, "Well, we're here, ain't we? Let's go on up and get acquainted. That fire in there is cooking something good."

A huge bear of a man came to the door at the knock. It took some minutes of stuttering for Mac to climb the branches of his family tree to show Uncle Willis where their two limbs connected. The woodsman leaned against the octagonal barrel of the five-foot Tennessee squirrel rifle, hearing him out and calculating it all up in his mind. When the limbs had all been climbed the man lit up like a fat oil lamp and scooped up his nephew twice removed as if he were a rag doll. "Suzannah's boy!" Then he pumped hands all around and welcomed the four inside.

The outside was a lie to the immaculate order and Shaker efficiency inside. It smelled as good as it looked! Shelves filled with jars of preserves were mounted against the wall. Batches of herbs dried from the beams. A crock of yellow apples stood in the corner by the dry sink. That held rising dough. Dishes standing at attention on a shelf above rows of mugs in the cupboard. A roaster nestled near the coals of the hearth. And a pie — no two — cooled on the sideboard, honey-colored syrup oozed in puddles over the crust. Early Harvest Apples! Nolan would stake his virginity on it. God was beholdin' to one of the four, only reason Nolan could explain for such a miracle.

Men did not have the souls for such miracles, there was a woman lurking about. Uncle Willis called the ministering angel down from the loft. "Ester, we got company. Come here, Woman, it's Suzannah's boy, Casper."

"Casper?" the three comrades hissed to each other grimmacing. Oh, the depraved ammunition of such knowledge as to their comrade's middle name.

"Before you open your mouths," Mac warned, "think twice. Remember for the next three years I'll always be fifteen paces behind you with a loaded gun. If the Rebs don't get you..."

If Uncle Willis could have justly been called rough-hewn the woman that alighted the ladder was all pink calico and eyelet ruffles. The steam had ripened her cheeks into peaches and coiled her dark hair into ringlets that danced around delicate, azure eyes. She was a beautiful, miniature woman much younger than her husband — no older than thirty.

The four of them stared. She wiped her hands on her apron and stretched out a welcome to each of them. "It's not often we get any of Willis' family down here, this is a surprise. Praise the Lord!"

"Soldiers they are, Ester, from over at Camp Dennison."

"Praise the Lord, avenging archangels to wage war against the great Satan Davis. This is an honor! You must be starved. Wash 'em up, Willis, while I gather some more food for the table. They are as thin as fence posts."

So far things looked promising, Nolan was distracted to insanity by the pies. But a woman who looked like that must...well...Quinn would be getting his bath. In fact all of them would be making use of it to be sure.

There was more Lord praising while the table was set. Then another verse again as Aunt Ester prayed over a dinner that was already obviously blessed in the sight of God. "Lord, thank you for bringing these four, holy Crusaders to our door. You have blessed them with acceptance by their President, the blessed Prophet Abraham. Let this food nourish them, give enlightenment to their vision and steel to their muscle to slay the ass Jefferson Davis with the fiery sword of their faith.

"Shine your blessing on these Angels of Death against all those who raise a hand against them and their mission to unyoke the lost tribes of Israel. Awaken those black souls to the light of jubilee. Not our will, but Thy will be done. Amen." Aunt Ester unclenched the knuckles that had turned white with fervor, smiled, and urged them to dig in.

"Boy, Angels of Death! If General Anderson had such a speech, we would have signed up for life." Nolan hissed and Quinn kicked him under the table.

"Your second piece of pie is mine for that."

Nolan peeked over the steaming pots to Christie whose eyes were rolling back in his head in ecstasy. The

94

biscuits tore away like tufts of cotton, steam rising in a cloud to be quenched with pats of butter. It had not been chicken but pheasant with chestnut stuffing. Gravy poured over fat yams. Mrs. Willis encouraged them to fill up on seconds and they did not insult her with demure forks.

If Aunt Ester only knew the blasphemy the Camp Dennison Quartermaster inflicted on God's heavenly bounty, she would add the demon Quartermaster General Montgomery Meigs to her list of the dammed. "Do you eat like this all the time, Uncle Willis?"

"Your Aunt likes to keep me fat so that I don't wander too far off. What can you tell me about the goings on in western Virginia? I hear old man Kelley gave them a lick and a promise."

"Yep, the Confederates quite literally took to the hills. Digging in up there now. Probably another battle before long."

Uncle Willis and the boys sat at the table and finished off the pie. After his wife ascended to the loft for the night, the older man leaned forward, "I used to have a little bracer for after dinner but Ester don't abide spirits. Said God can't speak to a fermented soul. Poured it out — even what I keep to relieve the lumbago. So I don't have anything to offer you fellows. "

"That meal needs no chaser, Mr. Willis." Christie pulled a deck of cards from his pocket and began to shuffle. The host recoiled as if his guest were twirling a loaded pistol. "God, man, don't let Ester see you with those. She can't abide the sin — said that cards are Satan's own bible." Uncle Willis hastened them good night and mounted the ladder.

Christie folded up his cards and stuffed them out of sight. The boys looked at each other and around the pristine cabin. "Well I said he was a black sheep. Anyhow they invited us into their home and fed us royal."

Quinn patted the little Scot on the back. "You are salvation itself, Casper, me lad. We are in your debt. Even if these barbarians are ungrateful, I praise you. Now if there are no objections let's get some sleep and see what tomorrow brings."

The morrow brought clouds of rain, and the day after, and the day after that. The boys huddled down in the oversized flannel shirts and breeches, Uncle Willis' extras, as Aunt Ester repaired the substandard workmanship of their uniforms. With each stitch she blasted the scurrilous bureaucrats and contractors that insulted a soldier's patriotism with such rubbish.

The four sat at the table, the unremitting deluge holding them hostage. Ester entertained them with Bible readings, prayers for the heinous death of Jefferson Davis, his family, his administration, the whole South and every heretic in the border states that wouldn't stay up all night with candles flaming over Bibles for the sole purpose of praying for the Union.

Four men who had shared a tent and lived identical lives suddenly had become strangers with nothing in common to talk about. The rain pounded against the cabin as each day of their furlough ticked away, and they just looked at each other. The cards tugged in Christie's pocket. When they could tolerate the incarceration no more, he motioned his comrades to the barn for a little fifty-two card revival of their own. They huddled back in the stall behind the cow and even Quinn blessed the proceedings by cutting the cards.

On the sixth day the clouds parted just as the sun set. The four comrades with barely a thin thread to keep their sanity stitched, pleaded a little air and a walk--just to keep their marching legs limber. With hands in the pockets of the huge pants the three tramped and slipped down the wagon path toward the river. Over three miles of mud and tangle, none spoke of the tomorrow that called them back to camp.

The road broke like the mouth of a tunnel onto a crossroads marked by the Red Bull Tavern — a poor excuse for a harbor. But there were lights glowing from the windows and laughter and cigar smoke flushing out the door as it opened and closed. Christie heard a deck shuffle. If God did not bless sin, at least He understood man's need for an occasional indulgence in it.

"What do you think?"

"I bet there's whisky in there." Mac licked his lips.

"And swearing. God, how I've missed it!" Nolan pulled them forward.

Quinn held back. "These places attract rough characters. Don't you think we are out of our element?"

"Camp Dennison ain't no boy's school. We whipped the Germans, didn't we? How bad can it be?"

"We didn't whip no Germans if you remember." Quinn corrected Nolan's memory. "The only reason we didn't end up dead or in the guard house is because of a lie so preposterous that it even made a lawyer speechless."

"You told it as I remember." Nolan dared.

"Come on, Quinn, there are four of us and we'll stay together. We'll even make Nolan behave. And we won't tell your Mom." Mac patted his friend on the shoulder.

"Then again," Nolan pushed back the blonde thatch that had grown down around his ears. "We can go back to the cabin. Aunt Ester should just about be getting out the Bible for another go round with the Philistines."

Quinn bolted to the front of the line and the boys fell in behind. At the steps they joined a file of other men making for the door. The leader tapped a signal in two, four-part knocks and it swung open.

It was a rough tavern with four long trestle tables two on each side of a center aisle, the benches were nearly filled with drinkers. A throng milled around the tap waiting for mugs of ale. They were passed back in lapping, frothing splashes. Quinn drew up short, "Any of you bring any money?"

A stunning oversight evident by three blank stares. "In my uniform."

As the four considered their embarrassment a burly men hoisting ten steins--five to a hand--dealt four pints to the newcomers, "For the cause, Lads. Welcome to the cause."

Ready to drink to the long life of such a generous cause they nodded, disentangled the mugs and passed them around. "You gentlemen better find a seat, the show is about to start." Nolan imbibed, the scorching liquid burned a path all the way to his stomach. "Oh!" he gasped. "That's feisty?"

A pint of apple jack and a show, a last day's reprieve for the small detachment of Company C. The four found a half-log bench against the back wall and eased back. The door opened and closed but no one noticed the strangers in their hurry to the bar. Oil lamps smoked and swayed from the ceiling emitting a scorching taste to the air. Although the tavern was crowded there couldn't have been twenty or thirty men--some in the rough uniform of tradesmen and farmers, a few in black-frock coats. The fire crackled and a black boy kept it stocked with logs against the late spring dampness.

A wad of tobacco narrowly missed Quinn's shoe. It hissed as it struck the hot bricks. "Sorry, Friend."

Quinn pulled his feet under the bench and turned towards the shouts for order. "Can we have some quiet, Gentlemen?" Wearing the black broadcloth coat of a preacher, the speaker strode to the center of the aisle and raised his tankard, "Let us stand, Gentlemen, and drink to the new nation."

In a clatter the attended stamped to their feet and raised their pints in salute, "The Confederacy!"

Quinn frowned. The other three exchanged confused glances but rose on cue and did likewise.

"Not going to drink, Friend?" The spitter was regarding him smartly, rolling another plug into his left cheek.

"As I see fit." Quinn saluted and took a cautious swig of the mysterious contents that smelled like apple juice but exploded in his mouth like dynamite. The challenger returned the salute and drank.

"Be seated, Gentlemen, and let us get to work." From his pocket the master of ceremonies pulled out a yellow paper and began, "I have a letter from Mr. Jacob Thompson, formerly Secretary of the Interior until his conversion to the one true cause, and now special envoy to Mr. Davis. He enlists our assistance. You see we are in the right time and place to render service to the Confederacy as valuable as if we shouldered a gun or pulled a lanyard. The speaker raised the paper in front of him and centered himself under a smoking lantern.

"You see, the western Virginia counties are in danger of being lost to Yankee invasion. If western Virginia is severed we lose the Ohio River and the railroad. The Yankees will be upon us in Richmond. They have taken Philippi over the prone bodies of our brave lads who made a martyr's stand in the streets. Our boys held against the blue demons inch by inch with their blood. Only after murderous fire was brought to bear on our valiant troops did they fall back fighting all the way. Gentlemen, three cheers for our valiant forces in western Virginia!"

The tavern exploded.

"That ain't how I heard it." Nolan hissed.

"Now vengence is mine, sayeth Mr. Davis." The speaker chortled.

"Mr. Vallandingham, we are yours to command." A farmer stood waving his arms whipping up a whirlwind of shouts. "Order us how you may wish!" More thunderous applause.

"Copperheads," Quinn exhaled. Nolan had read him of the Confederate sympathizers in the Cincinnati papers. In polite circles they were called Peace Democrats, but the troops called them traitors. They were led by a rabid, little, Ohio lawyer Clement Vallandingham. Events heated up.

The speaker threw the gauntlet down. "Our valiant men have fallen back to the mountains and the Yankees are thick on their trail. The Cause is in mortal danger. Gentlemen, we cannot let that happen. We must not let that happen! Gentlemen. Are you with me?"

The smokey, greasy air crackled. The spitter stole glances at the four not demonstrating proper evangelism.

"This is what we are to do. We must distract the Yankees from western Virginia by giving them something else to fight right in their back yard. We cannot syphon troops away from our valiant men at Laurel and Rich Mountains and Richmond has none to send us. It is up to us, Gentlemen, to distract the Yankees by...what shall we call it...a little mischief right here in Cincinnati.

"I have orders here," he raised a paper to quiet the roar," from Richmond to fire the arsenal, raid the commissary wagons at Camp Dennison, fire the railroad depot, and strike the Covington Bridge. We will strike, Gentlemen, like fox in the night, fire our targets and melt away in the morning sun. I have the authority to appoint captains and have chosen four

— each a brave, loyal son of the South, each with a special mission. Missers Tagers, Wright, Warner, and Lawrence — raise your hands, Gentlemen, so your soldiers can see where you are.

"Each man has his orders. We will set Cincinnati on its ear. We will make Lincoln's head spin. We will throw the Union on its back? Are you with me, Gentlemen? Who is with me?"

Insurgency thundered in chorus to the lightning streaking daylight and thunder outside. Men nearly tore over the benches, mounting the tables to raise their steins. "Then let us to it!"

They slapped each other on the back and moved to the four corners of the tavern where leaders waited to organize their bands. The four soldiers knew that they had to break out or their reluctance would soon be challenged. Slowly they rose and turned to the door only inches from Mac's elbow. Barring it was the spitter. "Leaving so soon, Gentlemen?"

"Just stepping out to get some air," Quinn slapped the big man good naturedly on the shoulder as Mac passed behind and kicked open the door. In a single motion the other three heaved the man through and Mac slid it shut.

Once in motion the huge man was hard to stop. The three rolled off the porch and into the muddy road. They struggled to their feet, the Copperhead crouched to pounce, "You're spies, filthy Union spies."

"You're crazy!" Mac struck from behind covering the man's mouth with his hands. Any alarm was overwhelmed by the break of thunder. Inside were enough fevered Copperheads to hang them all. The four made their decision instinctively to fight it out.

It took three to hold the Copperhead down as Nolan

released the horses and tore off the halters to tie him up. As lightning streaked just over their heads, the horses bolted around them. Christie yelped as the big man sunk his teeth sunk into his arm. Two had not enough strength to hold him and Quinn and Mac were tossed aside. As the Copperhead lunged for Nolan's throat, Christie reached for one of the rocks that edged the tavern grounds. He stepped up from behind and in a sweeping arc he brought it down with all his might.

The Copperhead lay at their feet. A puddle behind his left ear ran red.

Nolan pressed a finger to the palm and put his head close to the man's face. "He's dead."

Christie dropped the rock. "I wonder how he knew we were..."

"The shoes, Christie...we're wearing Brogans. Might as well wear a sign we're soldiers." Nolan looked at the door." Let's get out of here."

"We can't leave him here." Quinn hissed.

"Under the porch." Christie already stooped to pick up the legs. Coolly he motioned his friends to help. Rain beat so hard it was hard to see where they were going. They rolled the body under the elevated porch, pushing it behind the steps so that it wouldn't be found till morning.

At first light, the four bid the Willises good bye, hoped that Aunt Ester's prophesy that all that was ill and grotesque would find its way to Jefferson Davis' door, and set off for Camp Dennison and Colonel Crawford with their intelligence.

XIV

With its veteran reporter Whitelaw Reid in Western Virginia covering Kelley's "Philippi Races" the Cincinnati Gazette had not the reporter with the intuition or the contacts to plum the depths of the scattered outbreaks of mischief erupting in Cincinnati. With more enthusiasm than talent the guerrilla bands struck. But they were no match for General Jacob Cox, who had the uncanny talent of placing troops in the right place at the right time. Before any damage was done the saboteurs were flushed out by the soldiers waiting in the shadows.

About the same time a tavern beyond the crossroads of civilization burned to the ground. Rumor was a drunk sauntered in, worked himself up in a frenzy with some local farmers, and shot out the lamps in a tirade against "that Devil Lincoln".

Aunt Ester silently blessed the drunkard but Uncle Willis thought the circumstances suspicious, there might be more than the devil's own hand at work. In his forty-some years he had seen many a drunk stagger *out* of a tavern, but never as he could recall, one stagger *in*. Strange...mighty strange.

But these events transpired in the absence of the four anonymous informants. The Third and Fourth Ohio Volunteers had been called up and the twenty companies huddled in drafty boxcars that vibrated their bones to splinters. The camel-back locomotive whipped the cars through the valleys and foothills into western Virginia. The power of the locomotives surged like a roaring dragon, thrilling farm boys who had never ridden a horse car let alone a train of such power and speed. The noon sun strobed through the open doors, the men crouched in the dark corners, collars turned up against the damp perfume of the previous passengers, U.S. Government Issue beef ration still on the hoof.

It was as cold as winter even in the first days of summer. Men coughed and wiped their noses as they played cards, read, or leaned back and slept. Some were getting acquainted with a newly-purchased Testament, reading its pages to find a path to bargain with God. The cars had left before Sunday services — the first time the troops had been excused since arriving at Dennison. Oddly enough some men had grown accustomed to them some how.

"We are on our way sure to Richmond to teach old Jeff Davis a lesson." Christie all but thumped his chest.

"Think so, General?" Quinn hunched down for another forty winks. In the dark, Nolan saw Christie anew. In camp a more genuine Christian could not be found. More than the other two, it was Christie who hovered over Mac, seeing that the delicate boy got the best cut of meat, shoring him up with his share of vegetables against the dampness and dirt that wore down his lungs. But the brawl on Sandusky Street — Christie had attacked like a lion. At the tavern, Christie dispatched the Copperhead with cold efficiency, then saw to his disposal and walked away without turning back.

Chase had talked once about such men — some white and others red, he had seen on the plains. They had the hound of hell in them. They ran to the scent of the strike, fought with a fiendishness that consumed body and soul. When it was over, they were quenched and pacified. He hoped Christie was not like that.

"Where else could we be goin' but Richmond?" Christie hugged his rifle as if it were a pet dog. In their intelligence to Colonel Andrews the four had omitted any mention of the dead Copperhead. But in his sleep Nolan still saw the dead man's face quaking in the lightning. And sleep wasn't the anesthetic anymore.

"Virginia is a big place and there is fighting just about every place along it, I hear." Nolan whispered. "Ole Ben Kelley treed those Rebs in the mountains, sure. There's that job that needs finishing. And things are heating up in the eastern part of the state. Someplace called Fairfax County, a Confederate captain got killed. Bethel Church about seventy good Union troops got it — a lot dead."

Quinn eyed him curiously, was Nolan second guessing himself? Unlike his friend ever to admit a mistake even when it stuck out like a sore thumb or a white scar. Never apologize, never.

"You know, Quinn, back at the tavern," Nolan talked softly not to awaken Mac who dozed at his knee, "I saw something I never gave much thought to. The Rebs are serious about secession. This isn't a bluff. They aren't afraid of us. You were right. Those men at the tavern proved it — did you see their faces? They had the fever in them, to want to blow up a bridge or a train takes insanity.

"The war's here. This secession they mean to have it and they'll use everything they have to make it stick. Lincoln's got Union troops in his dining room, and he's looking out his window at Rebels camping in Alexandria. Then there's things stirring up out in Missouri. Men are dead. The house is on fire." Mac coughed to clear an obstacle in his chest, then settled back to sleep.

"Ain't that what you joined up for?" Quinn dared.

"I don't quite remember why I joined up. It was another boy and another time." The specter of his father was fading now. "It was like I was itching for a fight with a small man, one that I could beat up and put a finish to it. But I've been reading a lot about this war in the papers and it's like trying to beat out a pasture fire. Put out the flames in one spot and they just spark up someplace else.

"I've had dreams of it..of being killed by someone coming at me with a gun. I hope it will be a gun and not a bayonet or worse a sharpshooter. Lurking in the darkness he sees you but you can't see him. But as you come on, he's loading, putting on a cap, and drawing a cold bead on you like you were no more important than a deer or squirrel or the like. That...that scares me. That scares me very much."

"You ain't scared, Nolan, you're a soldier." Christie was not scornful but impatient that Nolan was forgetting himself and spouting heresy. The Irishman turned to look at the countryside flying past the door.

Nolan did not cowar, but there was the look of a man who has been awakened suddenly. He was very scared. Not just of battle, but of battle fever. Would he too loose his mind?

When he was sixteen, he had another of those arguments with his father that was as regular as bread and butter at the dinner table. But this was just one too many. The rage boiled up inside him, the handle of the dinner knife felt cool in his hand. His fingers wrapped into a fist ever tighter until the blade vibrated against the table. His father stopped his tirade and looked at him with the first full admission of fear on his face. The disagreement had been no different than so many others but suddenly Nolan could tolerate it no more. He wanted it to be over — all over — to be no more fights. The boy tore away from the table, ran down to the river and vomited. Quinn had found his friend the next morning sleeping in the barn. After that Nolan would not allow himself to get angry. His father too realized that there were limits beyond which his son could not reclaim himself.

Nolan now ached with the hunger for some hard

work to occupy his mind, to be exhausted. The twilight faded, the mountains that rose up from the Monongahela stood like barricades pressing the train against the cliffs. The locomotive descended like a swirling bird down into the valley searching for a place to land among the cliffs and rain-swollen rivers.

Growing up on the edge of the great prairie Nolan had never seen such mountains, suffocating and at the same time exhilarating. When he finally fell asleep they were well into the part of the Old Dominion where secession was having a hard time of it.

"Alright boys, all out!" the drums sounded assembly.

"God it must be supper time."

"Are we under attack?"

"Shouldn't somebody be sounding mess?"

"Where are we?" Sleepy soldiers shook themselves awake, pulled on cartridge belts and readied for the emergency.

"You won't be needing your weapons, leave them for the time being." Chase funneled them out of the doorway.

Company C lined up, men stamping blood back into their legs. Grafton was not the same station that bid Colonel Porterfield an inauspicious welcome only a month before. The Tygart still shoved and eddied, the trees were greener and fuller now. But the outpost was full of troops, the materials of war were depoted in the train yards and politicians — more politicians than Grafton ever knew — teemed in the hotels and bars. That June the western counties had forged a provisional government under Francis Pierpont and they were hot to form a new Union state. Virginia was at war with itself.

The Company formed two lines, about faced and marched to the front of the train where the rest of the regiment was forming up. Off to a side, Lieutenant Jones, Sergeant-Major Chase and several non-coms were deep in conference. Jones punctuated his remarks with gestures toward a boxcar that had jumped the tracks and a tree here and there. It was clear to the assembled, even without an interpreter, that there was some sore work ahead.

In due course the sergeants organized the men into two squads to affix a block and tackle both fore and aft of the stranded box car. Ropes were secured around a couple of sturdy trees with Union muscle at the other end. Company C was ordered on either side of the car.

"Sergeants, take charge of your squads and heave to on my order. We must be most efficient. While this car is off the track the whole line is shut down."

"Men, put shoulder to the sides." Chase paced up and down, moving bigger men between smaller, evening out the load, quieting the grumbles.

"I thought God didn't want us to work on Sunday." Nolan grumbled.

"I got His Almighty's personal permission." Chase pointed to an opening in the line.

The heavy clouds opened in white fissures and emptied. Men swore. Chase bleated over the thunder and the cursing. "On the Lieutenant's order, heave over." The steel burned into their shoulders.

"It's like lifting a mountain!" Nolan gasped.

"Gentlemen, you must do better." Chase snapped. The men grumbled, flexed their legs and put their shoulders to it again.

"Gentlemen, will you be putting some heft into it?" Chase growled.

"As far as I can see, the trouble is over here with these puny Dublin boys. No muscle except around the mouth." It was Horse, and the men of Company I fresh off the train. They took positions between their exhausted comrades. Horse's hot breath blew on Nolan's neck and he gritted his teeth and braced for the next order to lift.

Nolan smothered a profanity. He ached in joints that he could not conceive of ever bending again, swearing that the load had pushed him six inches deeper into the cinders. His stomach cramped from hunger, and he was soaked with more blasphemous cold and rain for late June than God had a right to inflict. His shoulder was raw, it was near midnight, and he wanted to fight. And here was a guy asking for a repeat match.

"Well, if it's not the only Ohio company recruited by mules." Nolan hissed just as Horse hoisted the weight of the boxcar onto his shoulder and groaned. The car righted itself in line but not on the track.

Lieutenant Jones barked, "Privates Quinn and Giles, front and center. Listen here, Boys, when I give the order, you two roll under there and kick those wheels straight on the track."

Horse sneered from behind, "That's right boys, you just crawl under there and hope me and Johnson here don't have to scratch."

The two privates looked at Jones. If his election came up again... "On my order." And he motioned the two down into the river of mud and cinders. When they were in position, he gave the signal, "Ready, heave!"

There was a long groan, a squeal of metal grating metal. The car jerked and rose. "Now, Privates, now."

Nolan and Quinn dropped under the car. Jones held a lantern low and the two swiveled on their shoulders, their feet raised against the wheels. They attacked from either side and kicked, and kicked again. The wheels jerked. The two men stamped at them until they straightened. It seemed an hour. Men groaned. Metal whined. If the load came down prematurely and the wheels missed, the car would skid to one side or the other. One of them would be crushed.

They rolled free, Jones waved the lantern and shouted "Clear!" The car slammed back onto the rails. The troops let up a cheer. The Fourth had won its first battle. Horse and Johnson pulled the two boys to their feet, brushed the mud and cinders from their coats, and twisted their forage caps right as if they were pushing corks into a bottle. "Listen, Brats, you did real good. But then you got the easy job. Anytime you need real men for the heavy lifting, give us a call."

"You braying castrated..."

"What, Mr. Giles?" the chevroned guardian angel hovered at his back.

"Expressing my gratitude to these two members of the Olentangy Guards, Sergeant, thanking them is all."

"Uh huh. Put it on a cake, Private. Now get back on the train." Chase motioned to the door.

"Are we going to Richmond, Sergeant?" Christie was not losing hope.

"Richmond. Yea, Soldier, by the long route." Chase windmilled his arm as Company C double quicked back onto the cars.

Co. C 4th OVI
Army of Occupation
Camp Rosecrans
Buckhannon Western Virginia
4 July, 1861

Myra,

We have come all the way to be incarcerated in another camp. Camp getting to mean any field, meadow, or barn yard that sleeps a hundred horses, a drove of steers, twenty pigs and ten thousand men. After awhile, we all begin to smell the same.

First there was Fetterman, then there was Camp Elk Creek at Clarksburg on the 28th, then we marched six miles to Camp Ewing or as we call it Camp Starvation. You can see the accommodations do not improve. You will be glad to know that Virginia has as much mud and rain as Ohio. Except today, which is as hot as a frying pan and pretty soon we are all going to explode like firecrackers. Of course bein' the Fourth of July, the General wants a grand review, since we all feel so chipper.

We feasted on fresh beef — killed and aged about an hour or so — and still quivering when we stabbed it on our ramrods. You can have it red and bloody or burnt as charred oak. We also get what the commissary calls hardtack — a three-inch hard cracker made out of granite — good for a bullet-proof vest. Makes prime roofing material.

The people have made us feel at home. The ladies come out with bread and pies. Nolan is at his most charming with the ladies and we get more than our share. There is one particularly handsome lass, Anna, that casts a fond glance at our bashful private. But Sergeant Chase won't let anything come of it. He keeps us under lock and key so the

Confederates won't get us or worse a cantankerous father with a shot gun. But I think they meet anyhow.

General McClellan has arrived but not by cattle car I bet. Nolan says McClellan is a soldier waiting to be a statue — every inch the cigar-store general — braid and brass enough to shine like the sun. Even when he stands he struts. The officers like him well enough, but the men aren't sure.

I think our salvation lies in General Rosecrans from Delaware. Can hear him night or day riding through the camp, barking orders, seeing to this or that. Never sleeps. The men feel good about him, looks to our care as best he can.

He's a Catholic in the bargain, his brother being a bishop and all can't hurt our chances with the Lord. Religion don't soften Old Rosie up though. When things are not what they should be, his boiler blows and he can blister the brass off a soldier's buttons.

I pray you keep yourself out of the way of this fever. It is deadly and you are not strong. Pray for us, but I think we are in good hands.

Quinn

XV

"I bet General McClellan ain't eatin' this stuff." Nolan spit the bits of hard cracker into the fire. He took a swig of his coffee and washed out his mouth.

"I don't know, maybe that's why he struts the way he does." Christie grimmaced.

"Blasphemous talk for your commander. After all he came to place himself at our head and share our danger with us. Ain't you comforted?" Quinn's green eyes danced in the ribbons of firelight.

"Yea, we ain't seen hide nor hair of him since. I had a turn at guard at the General's door. Man goes first class. A staff and a detail of orderlies, cooks, barbers...silver tea service. Humph!"

"Did I miss the instruction on how to dismember this thing?" Nolan balanced another cracker on a rock and brought the butt of his Enfield down like a hammer. The tack shattered like a china dish. He brushed the chards of wheat into his cup of coffee. "I'm writing my Congressman about this."

He let it boil long enough to soften sheet tin then scooped out a spoonful and sampled it. It attached itself to the roof of his mouth and refused to come off. Nolan scraped it down with a spoon and tossed it in the fire. "Soap! I wouldn't feed my horse this stuff."

"Don't worry, Gentlemen," Chase passed their fireside on his way to some business with the Colonel. "We don't feed hardtack to horses. A horse is too valuable — costs the government two hundred fifty dollars in gold. You cost less than fifty cents a day and there are a lot more where you came from."

At least the Company was at war, such as it was.

Captain Crawford had taken them out on detail tramping through rain, woods and mud, up the hills through paths channeling runoff. They found evidence of Rebels but no Rebels. A skirmish or two that was all. It was Nolan's thesis that the enemy was like any wild animal, they would not find the enemy until the enemy wanted to be found. But it felt good to go through the motions — it seasoned the men.

Crawford kept the company sharp with duty and drill, and then the four had been assigned a more rigorous schedule on the picket line. It resulted over some misappropriation of whiskey rations marked for officers only.

The rain and cold were a purgatory and a picket reached a limit when even a firing squad was not enough to keep his shivering, wet hide at his post. The four backed away from the picket line a step at a time to a shed forsaken in the trees. It offered minimal reprieve from the elements due to a roof that leaked like a grate. But something was better than nothing.

After passing the night, they hurried back to their posts leaving a small fire still glowing in the rubble of a hearth, and a blade of hardtack forgotten on a three-legged table.

Two nights later they came again. The tack was gone, but wrapped in gum cloth was a piece of cornbread. Nolan shared it with Quinn. It melted like sweet snow in their mouths. At dawn they left a bit of coffee in a handkerchief — Quinn's last.

In due course they returned to find on the table a wedge of cornbread wrapped in a piece of paper torn from the book of Genesis. On the front was an inventory of Abraham's ancestors, on the back the following:

Yank,
Much obliged for the coffee, returning cornbread in

kind. No more hardtack. Cannot leave more as rations tight. Don't think me blasphemous about the Testament. Reading about all that begetting made a boy lonely to be home doing some begetting of his own.
Reb

Nolan pulled out his pencil and turned over the page:
Reb
Will leave more corn meal tomorrow. Will sell all extra cornbread and share proceeds equally.
Yank

One of the four took to checking the cabin as regularly as they could get away without raising suspicion. The partnership came to pass, the Yank left cornmeal and picked up the cornbread which he sold by the slice. He then left a fair share of the remittance for the Reb and a down payment on another supply.

The comings and goings of the good ship enterprise went smoothly for about ten days before rocking on some choppy waters over contractual disagreements. Nolan picked up a sliver of stationary filled on one side with gentle script: "I hope you understand that I could not go on any longer. It is better for both of us that I mar..." The rest was torn away.
Yank
Your pay was fifteen cents light. Keeping cornbread until you remit.
Reb

Nolan took out a scrap and wrote:
Reb
I was not fifteen cents light on last payment, only five. In that we are providing the raw materials and sales

force, you will admit we are of a right to a bigger share of profits.
Yank

Two days later the reply and one half the usual allocation of cornbread:
Yank
Either you are stupider than ditch carp or you are a pirate. You owe fifteen cents from last time, plus two bits this.
Reb

Nolan fumed that he would not be insulted by a Reb. "You want that we go and find him and beat him up?" Christie smiled. "Your options are limited."

Nolan nodded reluctantly. He would just leave the cornmeal and let the Reb just try and collect. Two days later there was one-half loaf of cornbread and a note lodged in a rusty cup:
Yanks & Rebs
It's my cabin. I take five cents on each transaction of enterprise conducted there-in. Took ten first time to get paid up.
Third-Party

XVI

McClellan was moving his troops — pawns at a time — away from the B&O supply base closer to the Confederate camps at Rich and Laurel Mountains where the Confederates were dug in. Porterfield had been replaced with Lieutenant-Colonel Robert S. Garnett, Lieutenant-Colonel John Pegram second in command. Pegram had spread his troops in an arc down the western base of Rich Mountain, his headquarters as secure as an eagle's nest atop.

Laurel Hill rose directly north separated by a gap at Elkins. Crowning that elevation was a gerry-rigged Confederate post insulated from attack by felled tress and guarded by a ring of pickets. It is ironic that Pegram commanded from Camp Garnett, and Garnett established his headquarters at Camp Pegram. But such logic was business as usual in the army.

In relays, McClellan marched six regiments (including the Fourth Ohio), plus six more companies, two batteries of artillery, and two companies of cavalry closer to Roaring Creek at the base of Rich Mountain. There the Commander paused to pour over his maps and morning reports dotting i's and crossing t's before moving around the southern base of Rich Mountain to capture Beverly. Effectively he would then have isolated the Confederates from retreat or reinforcement without firing a shot. This McClellan meant to do. But only with the assurances of overwhelming odds, backup to his lines of communication, and a go-ahead from a heavenly messenger would the General move.

He waited too long. Former Virginia Governor Henry Wise, impersonating a military commander, brought his small force west and seized the Kanawha River Valley right under McClellan's nose. Jacob Cox, a man of efficiency

typos

and determination, was dispatched to deal with the disturbance in the south.

McClellan was blessed with another able commander, the newly-minted brigadier William Stark Rosecrans who had come up from Columbus. An engineer who did his homework, Rosecrans operated on the principle that opportunity was fleeting, it should be seized at once and executed with all-out determination. The Delaware men cheered Old Rosey as he rode among them, now they had a home boy at the helm. While lanterns burned late in commanders' tents, soldier's stacked arms and bidded their time.

To sustain them over the long haul, trains unloaded crates and barrels of hardtack, salt pork, and shortcake that the unitiated might mistaken for brick. Like the rest of the Army, the Hessians were issued their portion of the rations. Unlike the rest of the army they weren't about to eat it. Swirling in their cook pots were stews stiffened with squirrel, venison, rabbit, a chicken, perhaps a sheep or a hog if a local farmer wasn't vigilant. If any commander knew McClellan's order about respecting civilian property McCook could cite it chapter and verse. It had been roared into his ears as regular as Sunday gospel since they left Camp Dennison. However, it had not hampered his promotion and the Colonel endured these regular dressing downs with the other responsibilities of a brigade commander. The Germans loved him for it and followed him anywhere.

"Gut, eh!"

"Sehr Gut! Forbidden fruit is always the most succulent." Nolan mopped up the last of the gravey with a biscuit. "Too bad we have to spoil all this with a war."

"War will find you, you not have to go find it." Tag stirred the embers and his tentmates Josep Karl and Georg

Brunner passed the cigars. "Seen enough of it, came to America to get away from it. It's like a plague, sooner or later it rolls down on you. But no war tommorrow. We go hunting, Giles, you come along?"

Quinn held back and Giles prodded him on the back. "Not afraid of the rattlesnakes are you?"

Quinn rubbed the white scar absently, and Giles rushed to accept for both of them. "We can't live off the hospitality of others without paying back."

"The guard." Quinn reminded.

"Go down by the River, up the bank. We go unless it rains. Eh, Mich?"

"Quinn, you can eat horse and hardtack and die an early death of gut rot or we can eat like kings and Germans."

Quinn's battle of conscience was not tested. The forage expedition was canceled. The war had heated up. A scouting party of fifty men from the 3rd Ohio organized by General Schleich had grown impatient waiting for McClellan to finally give them permission to leave. Finally Schleich sent them out on his own hook.

Under Captain Orris Lawson the men traversed rough mountain country moving single file through the narrow paths of Virginia wilderness. Unmolested, the party hiked deeper into the Rebel-held territory and then crossed the Middle Fork River. Just on the other side, eighteen miles west of Camp Garnett they were ambushed by Confederates hidden in the laurel thickets, perched on the embankments and secreted in the scrub that covered the hillsides. The Buckeyes in the front went down quickly--five wounded, one dead. The rest made a quick scramble for suitable cover. Lawson sent for reinforcements and waited it out. In the meantime there was another skirmish. The Captain ordered his men back to the cover of the bridge. Without being told twice, the men picking up their wounded leaving the sole deadman on the field and hastened for securer cover.

The Fourth and Ninth under McCook were ordered to their relief. Chase had sent the four troublemakers ahead as skirmishers to see how they tested. Nolan took the point and pulled them Indian file into the dark primeval forest. Giles slapped away at the leaves and vines that tugged and cut his face. One branch and then another and another through a green maze to nowhere.

Breaking into the open, they fanned out first in fours and as automatically as a parade ground maneuver widened into a skirmish line. Chase had taught them well. They knew what to do. The advance was actually two lines composed of every other man from the first. One lined moved up between his buddies and ahead by five paces. Then he stopped and guarded the advance of the alternates who came abreast and ahead five more. The process was repeated in turns, like fingers inching ahead of the regiment.

The stranded troops were relieved. On the otherside, the Confederates had drawn back and the Fourth moved in unmolested to retrieve the sole dead soldier. Nolan raised a hand pointing to a bed of ferns about fifty-yards ahead. Brass danced like stars against blue wool stained brown with mud and blood. Nolan clenched his teeth and swallowed down the burning bile that gagged in his throat.

A Union soldier — swollen and bleached — lay in the July sun. Nolan motioned for Chase, "Sam Johns. I think." Christie and Mac pulled off their caps in respect for the dead, "God bless, Ohio, it grieves for its first son!"

With a thumb pressed to the deadman's forehead, Quinn traced a cross, "Bless me, Father, I am heartily sorry for all my sins...life everlasting..." Then he looked up for Nolan's answer of an Amen. Cold blue rage burned in

Nolan's eyes.

The Fourth Ohio saw to the soldier's burial. The war was still young and Sam Johns was buried with full honors of drums and fifes.

XVII

Private John Boyden of Co. D, 20th Virginia shivered at his post, his fingers numb against the trigger of his smoothbore. He had come up with three regiments under Col. John Pegram to support the Confederate stand on Rich Mountain. Just now he was thinking of home. He closed his eyes and let his mind soar like a falcon over the Alleghenies, across the Shenandoah Valley, then floating above the Blue Ridge to the piedmont and home. Cold rain ran like knife blades down his back but a hot flush burned his cheeks. How long had it been since he had been dry, fed, warm and clean?

Captain Sterrett's Churchville Cavalry were out patrolling the Buckhannon-Beverly Turnpike to the west beyond the curtain of rain. The Turnpike wound below Boyden's position to form an angle at the Hart Farm. There, behind logs and mud earthworks were posted the Pryor Rifles led by Captain Williams and beside them the Upshur Guards. Pegram was sure that the enemy would attack that way coming up in a straight line from their camp west of the mountain.

Across the road was the small, white farmhouse of Unionist farmer Joseph Hart. The family had taken cover in the spring house, all except the boy supposed to be with relatives in Indiana somewhere. Boyden hoped so, but his intuition made him uneasy about it, the boy would make an ideal scout for the Yankees.

Boyden wanted to go inside, to get warm, get out of the wet uniform — especially the shoes. They had been wet so long they cracked and sliced his feet into raw meat when he walked. But he didn't want to go over there to the house. The windows glowed like golden lanterns — but he knew there was no solace there. It was filled with sick and wounded. Doctors worked with no medical supplies, rations, nothing since they came up. Where they could find room, men of the Buckingham Institute Guards huddled beside the wounded in cramped corners keeping watch at the windows. The rest were posted out front in the corn crib and spring house guns at the ready.

But it was the house that scared him. There was no ether or morphine to snuff the wounded into oblivion. Boyden knew when a doctor amputated. The screams seared the still mountain air like the wails of a bobcat. No soldier walked in nor out of the house of his own will.

Captain deLagnel, Garnett's Chief of Artillery, was moving up a six-pounder to support the cavalry down the road. Three other cannon were being deployed along the hill — one more in the field out front of the house to the limits of the Confederate flank to back up Captain Curry and the Rockbridge Guards.

Beyond that was nothing but an ocean of forest and laurel, rolling along the spur of the hill into eternity. That scared him more. Since last night, there had been the sound of chopping down in those smokey depths. Too many axes to count, incessant like the bark of a hundred dogs, coming closer hour by hour.

About midnight there had been the ring of the bugle sounding Assembly down there. That's when the axes began. Captain Skipwith heard it too and had gone to tell the commander. Colonel Pegram had ordered them to move to their present position high behind headquarters with the cannon. But Boyden was still uneasy, The pounding came on as incessant as a heart beat.

Captain Skipwith handed Boyden a tin cup. Coffee thin and lukewarm with rain. He nodded thanks and restrained himself not to take too much of the sweet liquid.

Boyden passed it to Patrick Farley, who had been huddling with an uncontrollable case of the shakes. Maybe the coffee would warm him a bit. Farley startled as if he had been asleep, took a sip then passed it to his kin. But Pat pushed it back with a nod of his head. Something about being my brother's keeper knocked in the back of Boyden's brain.

"Colonel isn't sending us anything." Captain Skipwith apologized, "Seems they intercepted one of McClellan's couriers — got word the Yanks are going to attack on the right. He's sending everything that way." He motioned below where the Cavalry and Upshur Guards were in position, guns facing west.

There Captain Higginbotham of Company A of the 25th Virginia (the Upshur Grays, they preferred to be called) had heard the axes too and gone off on his own to alert the Colonel.

"But the axes are coming from the south." Higginbotham stammered his rage barely in control. It had been his second trip to headquarters to warn Pegram that the Federals were flanking them. But Higginbotham was only a western volunteer, Pegram was a Petersburg blueblood, West Point, a regular. With an impatient wave the commander ordered him back to his command. "Mind your own business, Captain, and let me mind mine."

Sitting ducks again. And it was hell keeping the powder dry. So if the Yankees came upon them in this rain, it would be hand to hand, if they were lucky. If they were not, the Yankees, with forty rounds in water-proof, leather cartridge boxes handy on their belts, would mow them down like a scythe through ripe wheat. It would not take long.

Higginbotham and his men knew about the Yankees, how they had come through Philippi with rifles blazing away. How they flooded down upon them through a sufuric haze, rounding up prisoners before a man had a chance to see who was friend and who was foe. He had seen the colonel fall, mortally wounded. But the command did not splinter. He wondered if the man died.

Higginbotham had turned with the rest of his men. Taking to the rear had galled him, humiliated him. The Virginians must have read it in the papers, the Yankees must have laughed. Pegram and Garnett regarded them as inferior material indeed, spooked by ghosts in the dark. Pegram did not have to worry, they were done running. They would hold here to the last man.

It must be beyond noon now, but the dark clouds hung so heavy that it seemed like late evening. The rain and fog drifted up from the valley on gossamer clouds. No fires. No coffee. The axes pounded.

Ben Gorrell huddled beside Higginbotham, and Henry C. Jackson next to him. Willis Woodley buttoned the cape of the blue military great coat that his cousin had sent him from Kansas. Although it was of Federal issue, Higginbothom had let the lad keep it. At the moment the greatest enemy was the cold.

Hunger had gotten the better of Jackson; he pulled out a candle and began to shave it with his knife. He slipped the chips into his mouth and sucked on them. The animal tallow and wax would confuse his stomach for awhile, but later the cramps made a man scream.

"Yanks from the South! Yanks from the South!" The crack of muskets along the picket line brought the 25th to the alert. They watched a line of smoke rise from the perimeter. When the Blue Coats erupted over the crest the Confederates hunkered down behind their guns to hold their line. The Yankees came on at the double quick up to the crest.

The Rockbridge Guards dug in. Breath came is

125

hungry pants so hard they almost inhaled the powder from the paper cartridges they tore open with their teeth. They filled the barrel, rammed the ball down, affixed the cap, and pulled back on the hammer and waited for the order to fire. They did not have to wait long.

Cannons boomed from the hill, deLagnel and his artillery pulled the guns through the mud. Union skirmishers broke through the woods, firing down on the line. DeLagnel slowed them with spherical shot and shortened fuses. Shells burst over their heads. Officers shouted to close up ranks.

Confederate support was coming up. deLagnel worked his cannon at the rate of four shots per minute and the Yanks withdrew.

Confederates cheered, all except the militia. They dried out their barrels and reached down into their pockets for powder. Pegram charged down on the line. "Can you hold, Captain?"

Higginbotham raised his sword and turned to his men, "Try us! Try us!" Pegram saluted and rode off. The cannon on the hill had mistaken their own cavalry for the enemy and were firing on it. He must see about it.

The Yanks came on again. Union shot caromed into the trees above them sheering the branches and raining sharp splinters down on the battery. They could not see the advancing Federals through the curtain of rain.

"Fire into the smoke of their muskets," deLagnel ordered. Spherical shot arced over the line of Confederates into the woods as fast as he could get it off. The cannoneers heaved the swab down, then the cartridge with powder and bag and shot, then the primer, and then the rammer again. It was a clumsy dance in the mud and rain. The lanyard was pulled and the cannon belched flame and recoiled.

The Yanks again withdrew. A roar like a tornado rose

from the throats of the line. Forgetting their hunger and cold, the Confederates cheered throwing hats into the air. Higginbotham did not cheer yet. He tightened his grip around his sword and motioned for his men to keep a keen eye to the South.

The officer was right. Three more columns attacked on the flank to the west, another threatening to cut them off. Federals aimed for the artillery horses bringing up the caissons. The horses reared and tore away taking the precious ammunition with them.

Confederate fire rang from the Hart House windows and from the corn crib. The Federals came on in a blue wave driving them out. "The Yanks took the hospital. Here they come! Here they Come!"

Higginbotham raised his sword. "Ready, men." A shell burst beside him and he saw Henry Jackson clutching his throat, blood pulsating between his fingers. Higginbotham gave the order to fire just as the first line of Federals surged over the crest.

The Yankees aimed on the cannon above, shooting deLagnel's horse out from under him. One by one the cannoneers dropped, May's left arm shattered. Ryder lay on his back, eyes open to the driving rain. One man huddled under the cannon propelled there by the force of the shot that crippled his thigh. Another had lost the battle for consciousness and collapsed bleeding from the head and breast.

With nearly all his men down deLagnel took a position at the gun ordering the two lone survivers to fire. As the last charge flamed from the barrel, deLagnel rebounded and winced. Blood poured from his hip and William Broyles, the last artilleryman left, dragged his captain to safety behind the gun carriage.

Woodley bolted to a fat tree the cape of his blue coat trailing behind him like a comet. A Federal drew a bead on him, lowered his rifle for a precious instant, unsure whether he was friend or foe. Reinforcements from Camp Garnett were going into line against the Union right but it was not enough.

The Federals came up in six columns, flanking the Confederates and cutting them off. Pegram had no choice but to order his men to fall back to Laurel Hill. Boyden wrapped an arm around his comrade, hoisted him to his feet, and pushed through the thickets. He shouted for the others to follow. The exhausted command closed around him ready to follow this last shred of leadership. The Federals did not pursue.

Pegram reined up and demanded to know the whereabouts of Captain Skipwith. Boyden stared at the commander for some time, then motioned back to the line where the Captain lay dead. Captain Higginbotham had been wounded as had Captain Curry. The three companies were without their commanders.

The mile-long retreat staggered on for eighteen hours. Men collapsed and disappeared into the thick bush. Comrades summoned their last strength to retrieve friends and pull them along. Another would drop only to be mounted between the shoulders of two saviors he did not even know. It did not matter, they moved on in the dark closed tight against straggling, yet they were picked off by Union skirmishers.

Pegram searched for some road that would lead his army to a safe haven. At Leading Creek Road a group of citizens advised the Colonel that Garnett had already retreated and was being pursued by Federals. The citizens cooked what rations they could for the ravenous troops. The

Colonel pondered the Seneca Road, only route leading to Beverly. But it passed over cliffs and through wild country. Barren of farms, nothing grew there but scrub and laurel. It could not sustain his wounded, exhausted troops.

When Pegram returned, he found them in panic. Sure they were surrounded soldiers were firing into the darkness at phantom Federals. They were wild with hunger, and exhaustion. Pegram reined up his horse and took out his pad to write a request to surrender.

XVIII

Rain stung like lashes of a whip. The Fourth smelled like a regiment of wet sheep. Could it be possible that more rain could make a saturated man wetter? But with every downpour there was another level of misery, cold, and fatigue.

Lieutenant Poe, McClellan's engineer, had taken out the Fourth to reconnoiter the area and found a ridge running along Roaring Creek and up the south face of Rich Mountain. He estimated that a position there would put them in front and south of the Confederate lines. Furthermore, Federal cannon once mounted up there could pound some heavy damage on the Confederate works. But it would take a road and men to clear it and it would have to be done quickly.

McClellan listened to any sensible plan that would avoid a general assault up hill. The road seemed the best bet. The Fourth Ohio put down their muskets and picked up axes to find Poe's road laying beneath several centuries of primal vegetation.

The ink was hardly dry on the engineer's orders when General Rosecrans with David Hart in tow brought McClellan even better options. Eighteen-year old David was the scion of the Hart Family, Union sympathizers, who had found their homein the center of Confederate operations on Rich Mountain. The boy knew of a remote path around the mountain that would bring the Federals to the rear of Pegram's camp. He had been away for some time but he was sure he could find it again even in the rain, brush, and darkness.

McClellan listened to Rosecrans' plan for a night march and a surprise attack from behind. It required a quick decision, not one of McClellan's talents. The two generals poured over their maps until a plan was agreed upon. Spearheaded by the Third Ohio, McClellan would mount an assault from the front as soon as he heard Rosecrans strike from the rear. A pincer maneuver — like its metaphor — a strike on two opposite flanks with the enemy caught in the middle. Rosecrans saluted, pulled on his gauntlets and moved out with about 2,000 men to see what he could do.

Deprived of a part on stage, the Fourth would do its best in the wings. With the Ninth on the flank the Fourth drove in the Confederate pickets blocking their way to where Poe envisioned his road to be. The rain beat down like an incessant ache that no remedy could ease. Men looked like turtles marching under their gum blankets, but still their uniforms were soaked and their shoes cracked. Chase riled at the contractors and Secretary of War Cameron. "Maggots, give their mother wooden teeth on a bargain, they would."

Like a brush fire, the line of men made steady progress against the forests. They moved with considerable speed considering the distraction of an umbrella of shrapnel sent over by the Confederates, and lightning from the Almighty. Through the night the Fourth bent to the job of chopping away the forests.

Five paces to his left, Quinn swung his ax at the double quick, relentless and indefatigable like a man fueled with vengence. Blood ran from scratches and gouges in his arms. With every strike there were new cuts from flying chips. Artillery exploded into the boughs above, raining down splinters and leaves. Slashing rain washed dirt and mud into their wounds, their shirts were pink with blood, their wool pants hung wet and scratchy against their skin, and their feet itched and burned in the soggy Brogans.

The strain was telling. "Quinn, you look.. uh...

perplexed." Nolan moved up to strike one more in the interminable front of trees.

"Me. What would give you that idea?" Quinn tore at the laurel entwined around another oak.

"And you too, Christie. I thought you loved working with wood."

"I'm a dammed carpenter, not a lumber jack. Keep that ax a little further to the right please or I'll be walking home on my knees."

Nolan hung his head in mock contrition, "You boys should be thanking me. You'd be just bug bait back in camp. Instead you're up here close to the action."

"Haven't heard any action except artillery and the lightning and thunder. And me under all these trees without my lightning rod." Mac rubbed an arm over his face.

"Touchy!" Nolan chastised.

"Think so?" Quinn was ready to settle some accounts, and this was as good a time as any to take inventory. "About two months ago you came over to my farm and I was doin' about this same thing as I recall. Said that what I was doing was boring. You said I needed some excitement in my life — let's go hunt Rebels. You filled my head with visions about the Army, getting away, seeing new country, skedaddling Rebs. I joined up. Then you almost left me high and dry at the recruiter's table because you were a few months shy of the limit. But we got in and you carried on like you won some damned contest. Only it wasn't just for ninety days, no for a damned life time — or three years which ever comes first.

"As I recall. We got in a fight not ten minutes out the door. Do I remember right? I think so! Not with Rebs, with factory workers with fists as big as cannon balls."

"Quinn, this ain't the time..."

"Naw, let me finish. I think I was on the subject of

fantasies. Yep, that was it. Well, as I remember events as they have transpired. In the two months since that night, what action have I seen? I have chopped wood at Camp Jackson. Then when we got things just about liveable they moved us out, leaving everything sweet and cozy for the new volunteers to just move in and set up housekeeping. Only now I hear they don't even have Camp Jackson.

"But then the Army moved us down to Camp Dennison, and what did we do? Now, I remember! We chopped wood. We chopped wood for barracks, we chopped planks for floors for the officers, for cook fires; yep hardly a day went by without some high-level chopping to break up the drill. Can't forget the little minuets — face right and left and all that. Let us not forget how I was nearly trampled to death learning that little waltz: 'By Brigade: Right Wheel, Oblique!'

"Can you only imagine the reaction of my mother upon getting a letter of condolence from Captain Crawford: 'You have my sincerest sympathies, but your son died a victim of an unfortunate parade ground accident?'"

All through his harangue Quinn had not missed a beat of the ax. He slashed at the tree as if it were the enemy. "But getting back to the wood chopping — I'm beginning to feel like a beaver. And more times than not we did it in the rain. Although this artillery is a nice new touch. Where is all the water coming from, I want to know? The firmament must be about squeezed dry.

"Did we go to Richmond? Naw! they put us on a train and dropped us off the far edge of Purgatory. And what did we do once we get here? But chop wood at Clarksburg and in Buckhannon and Roaring Creek! And who would Colonel McCook pick for *this* little venture, but the one regiment with the most practice at chopping wood in the entire Union

Army — why the Fourth who else. Would we be the ones to go up with Rosecrans — he being practically family — and scare some Rebs? Naw, we got issued axes."

A scar of lightning streaked down the sky and the rain which had been steady, descended in torrents. Quinn punctuated the celestial event with the first curse word Nolan ever remembered his friend professing. The dam had broken. Without a pause for breath or inspiration, Quinn went off in a barrage of cursing admirable for its range, vigor, and color — drawing on every word used by Sergeant Chase, the officers, and men, separately and in collections of descriptive metaphors that would make a muleteer blush. He went on sustained and unbroken until his profanity bucket was dry.

"You're going to have to confess that," Nolan hissed.

"God's going to have to keep count, because I plan to add a running tab before I get back to Christianity." Quinn stepped up to another tree.

"I never thought you would take offense to a few chores. After all you're getting paid."

"To fight Rebs. I thought we would be doing it by battle line, not digging them out of the ground like fishing worms. By the time we get done all of western Virginia's primeval forests will be firewood. And if I know Sergeant-Major Chase's passion for order, it will be cut, stacked in neat cord wood piles. I wouldn't be surprised if we wake up a couple of dinosaurs before long."

"We volunteered." Nolan watched the Third Ohio who had been deployed as flankers fall back. "Where they going?"

"That's another thing, Friend. I don't need you to volunteer me, anymore. I'm a big boy, perfectly capable of taking a step forward when and if the lieutenant's idea appeals to me. So the next time you are of a mind to volunteer us —

think in the singular."

"I...I'm sorry?" Nolan let his ax drop in mock contrition.

"Giles, I'll be thanking you to be talking less and working more. Like your friend, Mr. Quinn here." Chase had answered to the call of his name to see the little private dwadling.

Nolan blanched. The Third had been replaced with the Germans. As he marched by Tag waved a salute, "Gutten nach mittag, Herren," and slipped Nolan something in a piece of gumcloth, then kept on. Nolan unwrapped it, and his face awoke in a smile, "God bless their little Teutonic hearts."

The mutton was still hot. Chase was over with Lieutenant Jones. Nolan turned his back and casually broke the meat apart and passed it to his comrades.

On the right muskets cracked. And then the bark came in regular intervals. Rosecrans had engaged and the order to fire by file had been given. Nolan passed the hot food as far as it would go. Chase turned and set the axes at work with a vengeance. The men needed no orders. There was a battle on and they would not be found slow. The Fourth chopped through the night. The most exhausted rested in the rain without rations or coffee while those who could still stand guarded the road.

The crest belched. Thunder or cannon? The crack of muskets. The battle was on and the Fourth waited for the order forward to hell with the cannon.

"Sounds like a volcano taking the whole mountain top off." Nolan strained to subtract the thunder and lightning and the beat of rain from the sounds of battle. A snap of leaves and something stung his ear. Nolan slapped it and his entire head recoiled as if a nail had been driven through his head. His hand came away bloody. Quinn's mouth moved, but Nolan could not hear, words were sucked up into a vacuum of deafness. He thought he would faint and fell back against a tree.

"You've been hit." Mac shouted into the other side of his head at the same time pressing a cloth against the wounded ear. Nolan recoiled but Mac held his head firm into the rag.

"Damn!" was all he could say.

Chase came up, "You've been hit. You, okay, Boy?"

His head buzzed. Chase pulled the hand back, the boy's earlobe had been shot clean away. One inch closer... "It don't look bad, but you can go down to the surgeon if you want, Boy." Nolan shook his head and tied the ends of the rag around his head.

Captain Andrews reined up. "Old Rosey's being blasted. McClellan thinks the grand plan has come to not. Won't order us up. Blast!"

Morning broke on a white flag flying over the Confederate camp. "What's that?" The lead elements of Company C pointed to the flag pole where the Union colors would soon go up.

"A one-fingered salute to General McClellan from Old Rosey. The old boy did it himself."

XIX

Nolan stood guard over Boyden and a cluster of other Rebel prisoners. This was the enemy! Skinny, dirty, some in homespun, some in calico, and others in blue canvas shirts and rough-woven pants. A few wore butternut jackets, there was very little gray except for the officers. Most looked away when he talked to them, others looked back with filthy faces, hollow eyes. Automatically, Quinn and Nolan pulled saltpork and tack from their haversacks and handed it around. Honor gave way to hunger. The Confederates passed it without a thank you. Nolan and Quinn picked up their muskets and resumed their guard duty.

Garnett's command had made their escape, but Pegram had surrendered at Beverly and turned his command over to McClellan as senior and not Rosecrans. The Fourth felt some insult in that and there was muttering about it even in the face of victory. The regiment had been ordered to guard the prisoners until arrangements could be made for their dispatch.

Nolan regraded them, a fine bunch of skeletons. One prisoner coughed so hard that it doubled him in half. His sleeve came away blood splattered and his lips were purple.

"Call Surgeon McAbee and see if we can get some coffee." Nolan motioned to Mac.

"Don't be feeling sorry for them, Lad." But Chase nodded for Mac to execute Nolan's order. "They won't be suffering long. Heard the captain say something about parole. They'll be going home. Better off than us who will be here rounding up the rest of them."

Nolan adjusted the musket against his shoulder. They had been guarding the prisoners for hours to his mind needlessly. They were is such bad shape none of them had the energy to wander off. But Chase eyed them with venom. Hated this parole business. Allowed a man to rest up and come back to fight again. Chase confirmed the names on the prisoner roster and went off to headquarters.

"Your captain will get it all taken care of and..."

"Captain's dead, killed up on the mountain," Boyden challenged.

Nolan looked at Quinn, "Condolences."

"Should have been Garnett."

The sentries looked at each other, the prisoner spit, "Don't ever follow a commander who wants to die."

"No one wants to die." The ordeal had cost the man his mind.

"Garnett did. Family dead. Wanted to be with them. Sent many a good man instead of him. Too bad he got away. He should have died."

"He got his wish." Nolan whispered.

The private looked up. Nolan had heard the officers talk about it. "Died at Corrick's Ford, a few days ago."

A few bowed their heads, the rest were too exhausted to grieve.

Co C 4th Ohio
Camp Pendleton Maryland
Sunday 15 September

Dear Myra,

I think of you on the sunrise. When it is not raining, the fog rises in clouds from the floor of the valley and nestles against the first rays of the sun. It's quiet in camp then and a man can be alone in his mind to think on what nourishes him. It's the only time we have alone together.

The summer green has already begun to ripen into fall. We went to church last week and were blessed to meet the Confederates coming out. We exchanged salutations.

I pray that you will not forget me.

Quinn

XX

It was a succession of days, that proved that God was a good Union man. In September they had surprised a squad of Confederate Cavalry in a Petersburg church. The Fourth formed in line of battle with a battery to support. Captain Wallace of Company F was in command — a good Canton man whose shoulder straps didn't let him forget that they were all soldiers under the skin. He gave the order and the door exploded into splinters. Rebs poured out the front. The Ringgold Cavalry chased them down and captured some supply wagons just to make the insult sting.

While the Cavalry finished the job, Nolan and Quinn took their ease under a tree. Christie, his cap over his face, had already begun to snore. It seemed like a good idea and Nolan leaned back to do likewise. But his head bumped against a bough of mustered-colored leaves. "Oh!" he groaned. He thrust an arm back to clear away the bothersome log and...he patted it again...it was round but it was not a log. An investigation into the hollow unearthed a discovery of such remarkable proportions as to mark him a hero if not in the pages of history at least in the eyes of the brigade. A keg of apple-jack and another of stout. Mead fit for crusading knights.

Good news travels fast and this went like a hot wire down the section. Soldiers presented uncorked canteens. The crystal mountain water emptied for something more befitting the occasion. Captain Wallace rode up unnoticed to investigate. Taking measure of the proceedings that might present him with an unruly force to muster back to camp the officer bellowed, "That stuff's poison, Soldier."

"Yes, Sir," Nolan saluted, "My father is a preacher of temperance I know its reputation well."

140

"Uh huh." The Captain regarded the boy who still held the barrel and the privates clustered around him canteens at the ready. The captain looked at the men. They looked back. They had no idea what was in the keg, but they were willing to take their chances. There was the smell of mutiny in the air. The officer unstrapped his canteen and threw it at the private. "Well, I have never led my men anywhere that I refused to go first."

"Yes, Sir." Nolan filled it full.

The Captain smelled the contents and recoiled. Then he raised his canteen, "To Colonel Andrew! May he rest in peace." The men cheered as the Captain put the canteen to his lips. The jack cleared his throat with a belch of exhaust. His cheeks burned fury and he gasped. Wallace nodded and strapped the canteen to his saddle. "Now you boys won't be embarrassing me. We got quite a march home."

"No, Sir!" Quinn's eyes were already glassy. Nolan could see that his friend was feeling better of a summer spent wielding another axe building their new home at Camp Pendleton. It was a happy regiment that staggered back into camp.

Hanging Rock Pass and Mechanicsburg Gap were hardly important enough for the papers intoxicated with McClellan and his smoke rings of victory for the Army of the Potomac. Mac had been transferred to Washington to emerge the debutante of the season. Victories were only a formality away. He had all the worship a general could want — and men — an army to built into his own image.

Western Virginia was glad to get rid of him, they had old Rosey. And things were getting better. West Point Artilleryman Colonel John Mason took over the Regiment upon the death of their first colonel Lorin Andrews. Sam Carroll of Carrolton, Ohio, (West Point class of 1856, didn't graduate at the bottom of his class but darn near) coloneled the Eighth Ohio. Ben Franklin Kelley of the Philippi Races had recovered from his wounds and commanded the Railroad District. Rosey had been put in charge of the Department of West Virginia. Events transpired to make them cocky to a soldier who have ever sprouted brass. They had not only taken Romney once but twice, throwing Jackson back to Winchester.

Jackson took it out on General Loring for evacuating Romney, and threatened to resign if Loring weren't reprimanded and transferred. Instead of taking the two generals to the woodshed, Richmond appeased Jackson by sending Loring off to Tennessee.

But wintering in Romney was hard on the morale. The sleet covered the snow with a glassy slipperiness that crippled horses and men on the march. By companies soldiers grew sick. Pickets, who were not relieved often, lay down in a blanket of snow and froze to death. The body would be hacked out of the ice.

The commanders gave the order for the soldiers to take cover in what barns and shelter Romney could afford. Best accommodations going to the officers, mules and horses that drew the artillery and wagons, and infantry — in that order.

Officers moved into the houses — the hospitals into the largest houses. Companies took over warehouses and public buildings. The local citizens were outraged.

The Fourth found accommodations in the surrounding area of Blue's Gap. At the invitation of Battery B, Company C afforded itself the luxury of a barn, compliments of a farmer they did not know and did not inquire to ask. Farm animals were herded to a corner and the artillery horses secured. Men dropped exhausted near the battery wagon that transported the golden elixir. Outside freezing rain slapped against the wooden shingles to freeze on contact into every-deepening layers of ice. The men stacked arms and explored haversacks. Christie broke down a manger to start a fire under the eaves. He filled a bucket with snow to boil coffee.

Men with tin cups took their fill and collected in groups on the floor. Mac noticed the cow, her utters bursting to be milked. He moved cautiously around her, humming smooth reassurances to the tune of "John Brown's Body". The men watched to see what came next. Mac warmed his hands around his coffee cup and then put it down. He eased up under the cow and gently grabbed hold of the utters and started to pump. "Hand me your cup."

A private handed one down and Mac squirted a dram of milk into the cup. The private sipped his tan coffee and smiled. Someone found a bucket and passed it up.

Tired veterans leaned back to savor fresh milk — the first since leaving home. The war melted away and the bewhiskered faces of hard veterans mellowed.

The barn door slammed open. A bent woman swinging two pails strode in and searched for her Holstein. It chewed its cud contentedly now that the soldiers had eased the strain beneath. "What are you doing? You thievin' Yankees. Ain't it enough you take over my farm, kill my chickens. You steal my milk?"

Nolan stepped forward. With corporal chevrons on his sleeves, it was no longer boldness, it was authority, "Excuse me, Ma'am. The men meant no harm. Just a little milk is all. It's been a long time..."

"If you invading heathens had stayed home, minded your own business, you would be fat on your own milk."

"Why that old harpy!" a blue coat took a step but

143

Nolan motioned him back.

"You keep a civil tongue in your head!" She shook a finger at the boy's impudence, "Jackson ain't far off and he'll be coming down upon you like lightning down on Lucifer." She threw the pails in the straw. "Fill them up and bring them to the back door." As she turned Nolan saw the relief of a revolver in the pocket of her apron.

Nolan picked up the pails. "Mac, you seemed to be knowledgeable of cow tits. When you finish filling these, take them up to the back porch."

It was not quite first light when the provost kicked through the barn door. Soldiers staggered awake, reaching for Enfields. Lantern light shone off Union brass and men stood at uneasy attention, rubbing eyes and cursing under their breath.

Nolan moved to the head of the line. "Sergeant-Major?"

"Private MacGowan, is he here?" A lieutenant ordered.

"I think that he is." Giles had learned the first rule of command, never ever say more than you have to unless you know what you are talking about. "Is there a problem?"

"These men say he murdered a woman." Chase finally answered.

Mac reeled as if he had been blindsided. "I did what? No such thing!"

"Mrs. Hoage. Inside." The lieutenant motioned to the house. "Heard you had words last night. The husband said she was threatened by you. Know of any threats, Mr. MacGowan?"

Mac stepped into the torch light alongside his friend. "Only threats made was her makin' them. Little fuss over some milk was all. We almost filled one of the pails with what was left in the cow and made restitution with some script."

The lieutenant turned to the red-headed Scot. "Husband said you brought in the milk and had words. Heard shots. Thought it was Army business. Got up this morning to find his wife never came to bed. Found her in the root cellar."

"Never happened," Mac pleaded with Sergeant-Major Chase. "I swear. She yelled at me the whole time I stood there on the porch. Never let me in. Just stood there until she spent herself cursing me and my mother. God owes me for not sayin' nothing. Just took it and then I left. Never laid a hand on her. So help me."

Nolan turned to the provost. "How is it that they think it was one of us? A lot of soldiers around."

"This." Lieutenant held up a minie ball. Nolan examined it. "Taken from the woman's back by the surgeon this morning. You and Company F got Enfields. Everybody else shoots buck and ball."

The minie ball was not a ball at all, but a conically-shaped projectile — special ammunition for the Enfield and the Springfield rifles. The bullet gleamed like silver in the lantern light. The missile was mangled at the head, but the two deep rings around the base were still in tact.

Nolan stepped forward. "May I, Sergeant-Major?"

Chase nodded. The corporal was taking charge. Good. See how he handles himself. Nolan turned to Mac, "Your Enfield, Private."

"What?" Mac stuttered, "W-W-What for?"

"Just get it." Nolan urged gently.

Mac sorted through the pyramid of rifles. Finding his he handed it to Nolan. The corporal rested it on the butt and ran his finger inside the barrel. It was clean. Then he set the minie ball base down on the maw of the barrel. It rested on the mouth like a cap. Nolan pressed a finger over it and shoved. The bullet wouldn't budge.

Nolan smiled. Heaven bless the shabby contractors. "Lieutenant, the specifications say that the ammunition issued will fit both Enfields and Springfields. But it's just not so as we can tell you. Often as not we have to file them down and re-pack them. That's because our Enfields are little less than the proscribed .58 caliber — not much but enough to be inconvenient. If this were one of ours the rings would be shaved smooth and it would obviously be smaller to drop down the barrel."

He handed the cartridge back to the officer. "You know, Lieutenant, carrying two pails of milk would be all the Private could carry. Don't think he could handle a rifle. And why would he shoot the old woman? If he fired we would have heard it. And if he went inside that woman would have raised an alarm you could hear all the way to Richmond. Think you had better check around the family. I'd bet she was shot down in the basement where nobody could hear. And who would be allowed down there with the old woman?"

Chase smiled. Lovely. The Corporal had done fine, just enough authority to make an impression without being insubordinate. He turned to the officer, "Seems logical, Lieutenant."

The officer flipped the mangled ball into the air and caught it, stifled a smile, and turned to leave. Only Chase stayed behind. The applause was sweet but Nolan fairly glowed in the glory of one of Sergeant-Major S. Michael Chase's rare smiles of approval. It had been exhilarating to win the battle of wits, to have stayed ahead of the panic. But to have won a glimmer of his mentor's respect! Chase handed him a flask and Nolan took a healthy swallow. He motioned to the battery wagon. "Got something better. It can heat your coffee to a boil without even a fire."

While McClellan's eastern armies went into winter quarters around Washington, it was business as usual for the Fourth Ohio. They braved the snow and winter gales around Briery Mountain and Blue's Gap rounding up Secech. Prizes were Confederate guns, caissons and ammunition wagons. Colonel Carroll even found orders disclosing Jackson's movements. They torched Colonel Blue's house, barn and mill for giving comfort and aid to the enemy. Jackson was forced back to Winchester and the company was quartered for the winter at Romney.

XXI

"Listen to this," Nolan snapped the damp pages of the *Richmond Examiner* but it rolled down over his hands like a wet rag. "The Reb paper warns the Yankee invaders (that being us) that there is only one place hotter than Harrison's Landing and Satan's got the lease." He tugged at the collar for enough air to talk, "If that's so, what's that make the Virginians who live here?"

"Be kind." Christie ran a grimy hand across his glistening red face. The wet heat of the James River was too heavy to breathe and wore a body out with no exertion at all.

Nolan went back to his reading. Newspapers were the one luxury he allowed himself. Except for occasions of intemperance and profanity, he and Quinn were models of Christian rightousness — not for its own sake but out of financial embarrassment. Vice and indulgence cost money and pay beyond the barest necessities was sent home. They had even resorted to giving each other haircuts with catastrophic results.

So they did not gamble, play craps, or even race roaches for fun and profit. Visits to the sutler wagon and the tent of the "Pizancakes Lady" who accommodated those in need of feminine comforts, were beyond their financial reach. All that clean living was giving Nolan an unfortunate reputation at Colonel Mason's Headquarters as a model soldier, smart on his feet, good on the line. There was talk that there may be another chevron added to the two on his sleeves. The men respected him and trusted his lead.

Nolan had obtained the newspaper and a couple of books in a barter for some of the Cannon Shot. At the moment its fate weighed uneasy on his mind and he hoped the seals were tight and the load rode dry and easy in the hold

148

with the rest of the explosives.

It was the second summer of the war and after western Virginia's cold and wet, the eastern steam and blasted temperatures were a hell of a different sort. But the troops were happy to be on their way to Richmond at last. It seemed that the only army heading in that direction was McClellan's Army of the Potomac and for better or worse they were going along. "Send the Fourth down there and by next month we'll have Richmond on a platter."

No matter how Nolan squirmed his shirt stuck to him like a second skin and the four-button uniform coat heated up like an oven. Their new uniforms reeked of sweat and swamp vapors. They had been issued back in Alexandria where General Kimball had the gall to also order showers all around — no exceptions.

He was hungry but it was too hot to eat. Up there a little way was McClellan — a camp-sitting general they had thought they had gotten rid of back in West Virginia. "A statue, just waitin' for a pigeon."

Some of the passengers slept, others played cards, and the curious lined the gunwales of the ocean ship *South America* which had brought the brigade down from Alexandria. The wash of the James River all but boiled around the bow, the wakes foamed and slapped against the banks, tugging on moss, drift and refuse from Harrison's Landing. The flotsam and jetsam churned up by the huge twin paddle wheels made an ugly brown soup of the James. On the dead air was the odor of rot and decay.

A dense curtain of scrub oak and second-growth pine passed unbroken right to the water. Suddenly it would split apart like a stage curtain to present a sea of white tents, an acre of supply barrels, or a drove of cattle grazing beyond. The grand plantation houses evoked whistles of admiration up and down the deck. Nolan did not understand how a people could risk these magnificent monuments to the destruction of war. Something knocked on the door of his brain. For Virginians, Virginia was the "Cause" not the Confederacy.

Like Gulliver, the Harrison House was under siege by blue-clad lilliputians and their tiny, white-walled tents. There was a fuss of soldiers riding up and back in an impossible hurry. The flag of the Army of the Potomac hung limp and exhausted at the front door. From the left chimney flew the yellow flag of a hospital tent.

"I can bet you one thing, Nolan, me lad, those aren't our accommodations." Christie whistled. "Some people really live like that?"

"That's Berkeley, home of old Tippecanoe." Nolan whispered.

"Sure enough, it is." Sergeant Chase leaned over the rail, to relieve the weight of a load of army script deep in his pockets. It had been a very lucrative voyage. If God were not Loyalist, He certainly was a member of the family. "The breveted Lieutenant-General Washington himself used to call at those doors."

Christie was unimpressed, "Anything that old is probably inhabited by ghosts I heard tell..."

"Now it's inhabited by the Army." Nolan scratched the bristle around his chin. "I'd rather have the ghosts. Better company, they don't track mud on the carpets or burn holes in the furniture with their cigars."

The Corporal turned the page of his newspaper. "Well of all the nerve! We should have burned Clarksburg when we had the chance. That little Presbyterian bushwacker..." His comrades leaned closer. "Says here that Stonewall Jackson, huh...didn't get that name fightin' our

Brigade, and that's for sure, accused us of not standin' up to a fair fight back there in Romney. Could have whooped us, he says here, if we would have just stood still. And what was that little minuet he did up and down the valley...what was that? Fightin' or a Rebel quick step? Richmond papers aren't fit for the sink, already full of shit." Nolan balled up the paper and dunked it overboard.

"He's just a sore loser. We whipped Porterfield, him, Lee, Garnett, Floyd, and Pegram fair and square and kicked them right out of western Virginia. And we will whip 'em again if we had old Rosey. What you say, Mac?"

The little Scot grasped the rail. The massive legs that never lagged in the twenty-mile a day marches across the Appalachia had just given up. He slid down the rail like a cobra collapsing into its basket. Mac closed his eyes as if that would shut out the rolling ship, the oppressive heat, and the whirl of trees. If there was a benevolent God, He would just reach down and snatch his soul out of this miserable body right now. The half-dead soilder gagged and threw up over the side.

"Mac, you all right, Boy?" Christie eased the bobbing head against his chest. "He's burnin' up. He hasn't stopped this since we left Alexandria. Been sick before but not like this." Mac threw up again, his comrades holding him by his coat tails lest he fall overboard. "Hold onto him, we don't want to lose him like we lost Captain McMillen." As the ship was getting underway back in Alexandria the commander of E Company had slipped off the dock and under the waves. No one saw him again.

"How can he still be throwing up he hasn't eaten anything in two days?"

"Mac, Boy, I think Dr. McAbee needs to see you." The Scot recoiled into a ball. Christie slipped an arm around his pard's shoulders and leaned the mustard-colored face to his chest. For the blistering heat the boy should have been as clammy as a catfish, instead Mac's face was dry and hot. He trembled so violently Christie could hardly control him. "Quinn, get some water."

"No!" Mac groaned, his eyes bulging

"Out of the ration barrels. I just want to put some water on your face. You don't have to drink it." Christie looked up to his Sergeant for some help.

"You're sick, Boy." Chase pushed away some of the soldiers loitering along the deck. "We got to get him out of the heat. Pull him over here against the wheel."

Mac collapsed against the cool-damp oak of the sternwheeler housing and drifted off to sleep. Christie pressed the moistened shirt against Mac's crimson cheeks. The temperature was over one hundred degrees and his friend was baking like bread.

"No, doctor," Mac gasped deep down in his sleep. "He'll finish me off surer than the Rebs."

The ship channeled into Herring Creek. They were almost there when it began to rain. The drops vaporized against the hot wood and metal lifting another layer of steam into the heavy air. It was already thick with wood exhaust, glowing cinders and the suffocating stench of man and animal rot emanating like smoke from the camp.

"How's the little dervish?" inquired Davey Mahoney, the free thinker of Company B, 8th Ohio. He pulled off his forage cap and wet it down with the contents of his canteen. Mac struggled, got a whiff of it and relaxed. Whiskey! Mahoney patted the alcohol on the blistered face and Mac revived a little. He nodded appreciatively.

The diminutive Clevelander was among the gallant Eighth who had stood their ground against Jackson back at

Kernstown. In the confusion the regiment had nearly been cut off. They had plastered themselves into the wet, rutted earth behind a tree felled by artillery fire. The forward skirmishers of the 2nd Virginia came up so close Mahoney could reach out and touch them. But he was invisable behind the clouds of drifting smoke.

Mahoney would never forget how Jackson rode up in a hail of cannon fire to survey the ground. He seemed not to notice a shell bursting to his right. Little Sorrel was as stoic as its master. The horse remained planted to the ground until his rider ordered elsewhere.

A breeze parted the screen of sulphuric smoke. It was like a vision. Jackson set like Moses on the hill, his eyes burning like cold-blue flames in the midnight darkness of his face smeared black with powder and dirt. The General seized the hilt of his sword but the wet winter had rusted it to the scabbard. In frustration he detached it from his belt, scabbard and all, arched it above his head and churned the air for all damnation shouting for his men to rally and charge into the cannon fire. Mahoney's blood ran cold. Demoralized men, limp as rags, suddenly rose up as if galvanized by lightning and the wails of hell tore a hole in the sky.

The Brigade came up to save the Ohioans in time. But the Ohio private had come away with one impression. We will never beat the South until we have beaten Jackson. He is their archangel, their flaming sword. Romney and Kernstown was another time, he would not be defeated again.

Having survived Jackson, Mahoney had been delegated to the delicate duty of conveying the Eighth's condolences on the demise of the elixer — a battle casualty. The Delaware four admired heroism when they saw it. Jackson was one thing but bearing such bad news, well,

Mahoney was all right. Now he leaned back against the rail beside the five men.

"This would be a terrible place to die."

"Mahoney you worry too much." Giles threw an avuncular arm around his friend's shoulders. The private snorted. If the sodbuster was eighteen, Mahoney was Abraham Lincoln.

"Mark my words, Nolan, they can write all the poetry they want about McClellan. But he got this command because of McCook and Rosey and without them he hasn't won spit."

Nolan nodded, "Lee may have lost western Virginia, but they aren't going to lose any more. Something about all this that's sacred to them, nourishes their souls. Jackson ain't going to scare. He has blooded his troops; marched 'em through fire and ice and from what I've read they love him for it."

Nolan turned back to the rail, "Virginia is sure different from one side to the other. It's like even the land is your enemy...and the people...the women...the ones we met at Williamsburg. They hate worse than the men. The further we get into this place, the fewer of us going to get out."

"For what? "

"Huh?"

"Anybody know what we fightin' for yet?"

"The Union," Giles breathed. It's the only thing holdin' us together.

"The Union, huh. Let me tell you. Like your friend Quinn, my father fought for the Union — a united Ireland — back in the old country, before we came here. One Union is about the same as another in that men talk about it, fight for it, but there is no union in them at all. They talk about bein' free and of single independent minds. They may salute one flag, march to an anthem, but under it all, they are all different, as different as an oak from a willow, or Florida from Ohio, one dream from another, one day from another."

"This war is different."

"What makes it so?" Mahoney challenged.

"Abraham Lincoln, that's what."

Mahoney thought on that and nodded. "Yep, I allow you might be right. I guess he is the Union. He's different enough. West and east, rail splitter and lawyer, refined and crude I hear tell. Got a foot in all camps. Knows we're growing in every direction at the same time. My father took me to Gathersburg for the debate. I didn't understand it all but I liked him.

"Remember he was down in Falmouth last May? They tried to make a fool out of him — McDowell and that pit bull — what's that War Secretary's name?"

"Stanton."

"Makes an Ohioan blush. Anyway. I think God make him tall to stand above it all." Mahoney held Nolan with a long stare. "You willing to die for this Union of his?"

Nolan shook his head, "Fight for it. Dyin' won't be my decision. That, I guess, belongs to the Confederate who will pick me out on purpose or I'll be the luck of the draw."

Circling the deck to the bracing salutes of the crowded soldiers was a new star on the horizon, Brigadier General Nathan Kimball, late colonel of the Fourteenth Indiana and new commander of the Brigade. The old Indian fighter paused and looked down at the puddle of soldiers who had not saluted at his approach.

Out of concern rather than insult, the Hoosier stopped, "What's the matter with your friend there?" At heart still more Indiana physician than commander, he regarded the sleeping soldier with an educated eye and ran a hand over the forehead. Kimball leaned back on his heels and shook his head. "Get this man down to the surgeon and get him washed down in alcohol before he ignites. Break open the ration barrel if they have to. Tell them I sent you."

"Straight away, Sir."

The General stepped back as the four friends unclasp the fingers that clung to the rail with remarkable strength for such a sick man. "Let me go, you dogs, or I'll throw up all over you."

Nolan and Quinn each taking an arm pulled the Scot up taunt between them and started off down the deck. Mac would not be hushed and railed on in a stupor. "Where are you taking me?"

"To the surgeon, General Kimball's orders." Quinn hissed.

"Fucking Generals, can't ever let a man alone when he's dyin'. March 'em here...march 'em there. General should let us alone and go fornicate a cannon."

Turning the color of the setting sun, Sergeant Chase braced like a dam against the floods of profanity that washed back over his shoulder. The General about faced and with his aide continued the reconnaissance of the deck as if he had not heard a thing. He pumped a cigar as large as a pine log to keep from smiling.

He loved these men. Two steps away from the grave and the boy had enough vinegar to attack. Huh! You could keep those eastern swells. With these boys he could take hell at high tide. And it is not very often you get the opportunity to ruffle the feathers of a sergeant-major. Saluted with a snap and me not even a regular anymore.

"Yes," Kimball turned to his aide, "With these men we would show that arrogant, overstuffed, woodpecker son of a mainstreet baronet..."

"Sir? General Lee?"

"Lee, Good heavens, Man, I'm talking about McClellan."

"Sir, I hear that the Army loves the little rooster."

"What do they know? Never had a general worth horse shit." The aide struck a match and leaned to relight the General's cigar. "Give me that before you set my hat on fire. I've been lighting my own cigars since I was twelve, can light them now. Next thing, you'll be wanting to kiss my wife for me."

XXII

Wedged among commissary ships, gunboats, supply ships, ordnance ships, hospital ships, and troop ships all crawling around the wharf like beetles, the *South America* heaved to and tied up. Lining up by companies these veterans saw the chaos and the mud that was Harrison's Landing's main business. McChellan had been kicked from pillar to post from the Chickahominy River to the very edge of the James where his army clung to the banks for dear life. Nolan had over heard General Kimball cursing the dispatches. It was all true.

McClellan had brought his Army right to the very gates of Richmond, but lost his nerve when all he needed *was* nerve. With 90,000 men at his command and the Richmond church towers beckoning on the horizon, Mac folded his cards. He had been bluffed by a second-rate general and third-rate actor John Magruder — a dandy, sporting knee boots and bad Shakespeare. The wily Reb had trailed pine branches behind a few hundred horsemen running them up and down the Richmond roads, swirling up enough dust for a legion. Pinkerton wagged to McClellan that there must be 120,000 to 130,000 Confederates in there probably armed with lightning bolts. Nobody had enough smarts to wire back to Washington for a reading on the 1860 census. Kimball doubted there were that many males in all of Virginia included the mules. Humph. This mess could have been a long way towards being over if the "Little Napoleon" had any guts. Hesitation is damnation. Caution is the excuse of losers.

All Mac proved was that he had the makings of a good retreat man. Lee had brought Jackson from the Valley and with his 85,000 kicked the son of the upper-crust Philadelphia physician and his Army from pillar to post —

Mechanicsville, Gaines Mill, Savage Station, Frayser's Farm, and Malvern Hill — a good week's work for a general when you can get it. The papers were calling it the "Seven Days" and eating it up! No amount of cigars and brandy could put a shine on the press reports burning the wires back East. Kimball puffed on his cigar and took his ease. From the looks of it, it would be the last chance he would relax for a long time.

Finding exactly where the James River left off and Harrison's Landing correctly began was a subject for debate. The Brigade stood in ranks in the Berkeley wheat field, their shoes sinking down with every twitch. Around them muleteers waved whips and swore oaths at exhausted animals. Mules sat back on their rumps to wait however long it took nature to dry the ground out. Drivers in wagons sunk to their hubs cracked whips and swore some more.

Horses pulling cannon, limbers, and wagons, churned and buckled in the mud. Thrashing and naying in panic, the animals sunk all the faster until their hearts exploded and put them out of their misery. A drover tried to turn beef cattle that had strayed into the quagmire, only for his horse to be trapped. The only animal to save himself was the rider.

Malaria floated up from the swamp in the festering steam. The surgeons considered it poison to the lungs of men and animals alike who sucked it in great gasps. But it was the tainted water drawn from the wells poisoned from the run off and the ground water from the sinks, the hospital amputation pits, the garbage heaps, the manure and the slaughter pens. A man smelled the water before he could drink it, he gagged and vomited it up. The soldiers did not see fit to boil it before drinking it except when making up their coffee. It washed down the salt pork, rare beef, sauerkraut and hardtack until the bowels and intestines revolted. Harrison's Landing was a plagued village waiting to die by its own hand.

Impatient for orders to go anywhere out of the swamp, the men sunk deeper into the ooze of muddy syrup. When they marched, the mud sucked the Brogans off their feet like glue. Here were Kimball's western regiments — veterans of the 14th Indiana, 4th, 8th, and 67th Ohio, 84th Pennsylvania, and 7th West Virginia. They formed up with the pride of men who had never been licked to become the First Brigade, 3rd Division, II Corps, Army of the Potomac — an army that had never won. Like water and oil the two would not mix even with shaking.

Chase cursed. It had come to this. It was something to die in a fair fight, but to strangle in your own waste was a humiliation. He loved these boys, had volunteered to serve with them. They were a good lot, had proved it every lick of 'em. Deserved better. And what came after, scurvy and rickets, bleeding gums spitting out your teeth, shitting out your insides, the shakes. God save us from Generals!

"Welcome to the Army of the Potomac, Gentlemen?" Chase hissed. As the Brigade stood helpless on the river bank, Lee's cannon whistled shells over their heads. Most exploded harmlessly into the river. The gunboats in the James replied in kind. McClellan's army was falling back. Instead of going into camp, the Brigade was ordered to protect the last of the retreating flank.

Quinn and Christie took up their posts on the skirmish line with Nolan at the point. John Kendrick, replacing the ailing MacGowan, made up the fourth man. Chase had picked him, as he had picked the others. They would see if he picked right.

Extra rounds were passed and the rest of the regiment formed behind them on either side of the colors. Colonel Crawford raised his sword, "Men! We are at the front of the line. All eyes are on Ohio! Our colors have never been dropped in the mud of retreat. We are Gibraltar!"

Christie and Quinn turned to Kendrick. A look that a new man understands — fail and you don't have to worry about the enemy. General Kimball rode to the front, saluted his men. He drew his sword and arched it down the Charles City Road, the Fourteenth Indiana moved out on the flank. The order to forward march echoed down the long blue column.

Thunder clouds growled. Soon they forgot how miserable they were so absorbed in the work ahead. Men stepped up with the confidence of veterans, the skirmishers, vigilant in the ways of sharpshooters, kept a sharp eye to the dark hollows of oaks and sycamore boughs. A glimmer of a barrel, a cock of a trigger, a path of matted grass, a wave of grass in the windless afternoon, or a rustle of wildlife.

The coolness was a relief but the bugs! They bit and stung the face, the eyes, getting in the mouth. With ever step, a new horde exploded up in a cloud. It was all a man could do to restrain himself from slapping at them. The skirmish line drew up, the stand of timber broke into an open pasture. Bare ground, undulating like rolling ocean waves. Nolan stepped off and down into a mire channelling the swollen run offs. It ran warm as urine into his shoe. More mosquitoes and gnats swirled into his face sticking to the sweat running down his face.

He did not look down, the danger lay in the open land stretching before him. Cannon with infantry could be waiting in the depressions, invisible until the column was upon them. In a split second a line of rifles could rise up and fire point blank in their faces. Bad ground.

Hammers cocked. Squirrels chirped and scrambled to the far side of trees. A rabbit bounded into the brush.

Kendrick swallowed, feeling naked, "Run you old hare, if I didn't have a reputation to protect, I'd beat you down that hole."

Scrub pulled at Nolan's ankles as he stepped into the open. His thumb caressed the trigger of the Enfield. The sun broke through the clouds and boiled the sweat and salt into his eyes. The sleeve of his dirty coat cleared his face. The long blue wave was ready to follow him into the pasture. But Nolan kept the regiment in the trees extending the advance line a few paces. If there were Confederates the skirmish line could tease them out.

Nolan had been right. Less that a quarter mile away a line of Confederates rose up out of the grass and a line of fire flashed across the Union front. The order echoed and the regiment opened up a curtain of smoke. The even roll of the first round heated into a general barrage. Canister from the Confederate battery overshot the skirmishers exploding a deadly hail into the regiment.

Pillows of ashen sulphur hovered on the ground. Nolan shot low aiming at the men working the cannon behind the drifting smoke. He rolled over to reload, ramming another charge home and took aim. He fired and reloaded again and again in the cool rhythm of a veteran.

"Cussed!" his rifle fouled. He reached for another, wiping the blood away from the stock. Support surged around him. Agonizing cries from the rear told that the enemy batteries had their range. Calculated it long before the regiment had stepped into the open.

A cloud of blood and muscle sprayed over him. The 8th came up laying down a line of fire but their own batteries were still far to the rear. His ammunition gone Nolan hugged the ground and waited for someone to pass him more. It did not come. The battle was dying out. The last Confederate cannon fell back behind a thin screen of infantry cover.

"Damn!" He choked on the nitrate burning on his skin. "Get the guns!" Nolan pointed to the cannons that were shimering in the waves of heat and clouds. A line of Confederates held until the cannon could be safely pulled away.

The Fourth lay on their empty guns as the West Virginians and the Hoosiers surged passed. Victory was a handful of brave Rebels who sacrificed themselves for their precious artillery. The Union rush advanced no further than these few trophies.

"No! Get the guns!" Nolan coughed. "Chase them down! Get the guns!" Rifle fire trickled out like the last drops of rain, then it was over.

"Where in the hell do you think you're going?" Quinn yanked his comrade back by his sleeve.

"The cannon!" But Quinn held him tight as the 8th herded the prisoners past him — a ragged, tattered group — no two alike. The seizure to run down the enemy passed. Nolan swore. It did no good.

"Hello, Yank." An echo from Rich Mountain.

Nolan spit, "Hello, Reb!"

The prisoner sneered, white eyes and yellow teeth gleamed through a grimmy face, like a jack-o-lantern. "Greetings, Gents! I guess I will be partaking of your house-po-tal-ity agin."

"Move along, this ain't no reunion." The Reb doffed his ragged forage cap. Quinn kept a hold on his friend.

Nolan spit again. His mouth was dry and gritty. "Trouble with this army. We're too damned civilized."

Chase motioned for them to pick up their weapons and be of general assistance in moving the casualties to the rear. Nolan pointed, "Them prisoners. How long before they're paroled, exchanged and back on the line against us?"

"Christmas." Chase spit, "Probably sooner."

"Precisely. If we keep fighting the same old enemy over and over again, we ain't ever going to make any progress. Anyway it's the cannon that's our real enemy. Cannon we don't parole and exchange, cannon we keep, and they lose. No more check and checkmate. We need to play for keeps."

A mushroom of dust flushed as a forage cap slapped against his thigh. He straightened it on his head and moved back where the line was reforming.

Mahoney strode up his musket barrel still at the ready. "Nolan second guessing the generals again? Maybe Kimball will invite you to tea and discuss strategy."

"Easy friend, his fever is up." Kendrick, a veteran of many iron-town brawls and bar-room fights knew never throw stones at an angry dog.

The clouds broke open and cleaned the cannon smoke from the air. Soldiers turned their faces up to the sky to wash away the grime and dirt. Then looked to the wounded. Captain Crawford of Company C was born passed to an ambulance.

Kimball's Brigade had made its debut into Potomac society.

XXIII

Sleep. It did not come. The drizzle soaked them from above, sweat from within, mud from below. Tents had not yet arrived, not that they could have been pitched anyway. The ground was like pudding, too soft to hold the pegs.

The camp was a furnace. The heat had set the lice to a crawling frenzy, the flies bit so bad that they drove a soldier insane. And the stench starved the lungs for air.

Nolan turned, kicked at one of the pine branches. They made a lumpy mattress but at least he was above the swamp. He had just drifted off when swill seeped up his pants leg.

Cursing from habit rather than intention, Nolan could stand himself no longer. The fire was down to white charcoal. It would have to do. He poured water from his canteen into a mixture of coffee and sugar. From over his shoulder another canteen raised the level in his cup double.

"Chase says to boil it longer and stronger and you won't get the soldier's disease." Quinn's voice was husky from coughing.

Milk in his coffee would almost make it all tolerable. The sutler sold cans of heavy yellow syrup that Borden had contracted but it cost too much. In spite of the heat they eased by the fire. When the coffee was the color and thickness of axle grease, Nolan lifted it out of the coals and poured off half. Nolan sipped and waited for the coffee to kick in. Quinn pulled the layers of blonde wet silk out of his collar and scratched the fresh growth that masked his face.

"If Myra could see you now, what would she think?"

"What about you, that colleen from West Virginia set about writing to you yet?"

"Can't see why she should, she can't write." Had it

only been a year ago? Anna, the magnificent ruby, set in the lush emerald hills of Clarksburg! That was before Sam Johns.

"Got enough for two more there?" Two rangy Federals strolled into the camp light. The brass insignia of the 69th-NY glistened on the crown of their forage caps. "I'm Gerald Malone. Here's my shadow and very own cousin also Gerald, only accent on the last syllable. We allow other than family to call him by his Confirmation name Daniel, so they don't get confused."

He had a heavy syrupy brogue with a Bowry bite to it, "It's no rest for the wicked, Lads. Saw your boat come up from the picket line. Welcome to the neighborhood. Strictly first class accommodations for the Army of the Potomac. See you requisitioned a mattress provided by the forests of the good Lord. With this mess...wait till you get the curse of the pine beetles. It is something when they go to war with the lice under your shirt."

Quinn divided the boiling coffee into two more cups and watered it down. The two New Yorkers leaned back oblivious to the chaos and stench around them. Nolan smiled, of course they had made peace with it by becoming part of it. That was our trouble, the new men fought it — a losing battle in the end.

The two were both large, powerfully-built men, their wool coats straining to contain the expanse of muscle in the shoulders and arms. Both were fully bearded — one dark the other light — related like day to night — with a sharpness in the eyes that always kept a look to the rear.

There was no need for further family history, news of the 69th flew on the air like a hawk on a heated current. The Irish Brigade made up of three regiments — might as well be six — an army in themselves led by an Irish radical. Hell fighters flanking the emerald colors.

"I'm Nolan Giles, my friend is Brian Quinn, Company C, 4th-OVI."

"Kimball's babies."

Nolan and Quinn exchanged rude glares behind their cups. Quinn, took up the responsibility of extending pleasantries, "Quiet out there?"

Daniel nodded, "For the time being. But not for long. Stonewall is up." He took another sip as if that said it all.

Nolan and Quinn sipped at their coffee. Finally something needed said on the subject, "Stonewall ain't a tornado. He can be whipped."

Daniel glowered over his tin cup at the corporal, "That so? Then why didn't you lick 'em when you had him in the Valley? Then we could tend to things here?"

"I think my friend means..." Quinn tried to stamp out the burning fuse leading to short tempers. Retreat or change of base — that was what McClellan called it. It looked too much the same in the eyes of the men. They were sensitive to it, searching for fault in some other quarter than their commander and themselves. In the Division newly arrived from Shenandoah they had their culprits.

"I think I know what your friend means," Daniel Malone bristled like a cat, "that we ain't been doing our job out here. Next thing he'll be saying is that it was Mac's fault. But we could have cleaned this mess up, we had them at Mechanicsville when Jackson was out of the way. Who was it that let him slip clean out of the Valley? Any army worth its pay.."

"Look, Friend, I meant no disrespect. It's just that Jackson and Lee...well they are not some holy ghosts conjuring up troops out of rocks. They got the same problems we have, and with the right generals we could..."

The Irishman bristled, "We got more than enough

right here."

"You have been misinformed." Nolan answered evenly, "Mac's got the army, the cannon, the West Point certificate, he just ain't got the nerve."

"West Virginia says different."

Nolan cut Daniel off, "In West Virginia Mac had Rosecrans and Cox."

"And I suppose you..." The dark Irishman raised himself up like a giant.

"Yea, he had us." Nolan rose but only up to the Irish man's shoulder. The corporal rolled his fingers into a fist.

"Daniel, the boy didn't mean..." Gerald stood in front of his cousin, but he was shoved aside.

"Shut up," Daniel turned back, "Look, you..."

"Who you calling a boy?" Nolan growled and turned to confront the other Irishman not an inch shorter than his cousin. "We were in action before you guys even knew the business end of a gun barrel. We would have kept Jackson in the Valley if we didn't have to march across Virginia to be in a parade and get our damn, fool pictures took in Fredericksburg. Thank your Generals for that." Nolan pitched his coffee into the coals. "This little social is over so let's get some sleep before we say something..."

"Nolan!" Too late, too tired and too angry, Daniel grabbed the boy and spun him around. The seam of muslin shirt gave in a searing rip.

Daniel backed away suddenly contrite. An apology was ready on his lips but Nolan sent his right fist up like a comet under the man's jaw to cut it off. And he brought the left in rapid succession into the ear.

The Irishman winced, that's all. He took aim on the little terrier. Before the corporal could duck, a fist as big as a sixteen-pounder shell came out of the shadows. Nolan was lifted up off his feet and dropped only inches from white coals.

That he was well out of his weight class was only a technicality, the Buckeye wavered on unsteady feet ready to return to the discussion as soon as the camp stopped spinning. The Irishman assisted. Grabbing the front of Nolan's coat, he hoisted the boy up like a sack of flour, and positioned his pulsating head in dead sights for another punch when...

"What in the sam hill is going on here?"

"Oh my God!" Quinn exhaled as an officer with a star glistening on each shoulder strap stepped into the firelight.

"Not quite but close!" Daniel dropped the little corporal and braced to salute. The Irish did not extend introductions. If thunder did not announce his entrance it was God's oversight.

Quinn braced but Nolan still balanced on the ground as if it pitched like the deck of a ship. A broad-brimmed officer's hat with golden tassels shaded all of the man's face except the growth of beard on the chin. But they knew. Meagher.

"Sir!" The four men barked.

Quinn straightened on unsteady legs, but the officer was more interested in the two Irishmen. Power makes a man bigger than life and he loomed over the two giants. The General surveyed the damages as men held at attention. As senior it was Nolan who should answer but at the moment he was blinking at the blur that pulled and tugged at the General's image like taffy.

Meagher wore his frock coat buttoned only at the neck. Two, inch wide, gold stripes ran parallel down the seams of trousers to the cuff of blackened field boots. The general must have been on a stroll enjoying the last cigar of the night or the first cigar of the new day, because he was not dressed for business. The sash and presentation sword were not dangling on the officer's hip. But in spite of his rank and resplendent uniform, Meagher was remarkable because he was clean, buffed, and trimmed. Probably even had a bath.

The officer surveyed the casualties. The big one would be presentable in a couple of days, must have been taken by surprise.

Meagher growled at his prodigal sons. The rest of the Army called them Meagher's Exiles. He had taken to keeping them busy when not on the line with policing and extra drill. Dammed they were the best drilled brigade in the whole Army. But they needed careful handling, right now they were as touchy as firecrackers. "Well!" The General peered into the rapidly-swelling eye of the little banty rooster. "Do you have anything to say?"

"Corporal Nolan Giles, Sir, 4th Ohio, Kimball's Brigade."

The General turned to his companion and on cue, "Private Brian Quinn, Sir, the same."

It was imperceptible, just a slight quiver, something in the face of the second man had startled the General. He stood transfixed as if he had seen a ghost and for an instant lost his control on the business he had begun. When he spoke his voice was horse, "Yes, and these two gentlemen I think I know. What's the meaning of this, Private Quinn?"

"An accident, Sir. Nothing more, Sir." As Nolan's guardian angel, Quinn had come to accept these upbraidings as inconvenient but not life-threatening.

The General hurumphed. "Accident, Corporal?"

"Yes, Sir. Our acquaintance, Mr. Malone here well he was just..." Nolan thought better of elaborating. I'd not be giving him anything about a false step if I were you. Firing

Squad. Nolan paused to clean the blood from his eyes, "Sir, a misunderstanding is all... Sir."

"I see, Corporal Giles."

Behind him the sky was already fading into a denim blue. The men were miserable enough, they did not need a chewing. Morale was bad enough. But he had to do something. "Gentlemen, there is plenty of war out there. You men from West Virginia, we welcome you even if we're too proud to say so. But you've got to respect the fight we've had here. From now on we're all apart of the same fist — the same purpose. It's the only way we're going to end this thing." He drew on his cigar and released a cloud, nodded good night and moved out into the night.

When it was clear, Mahoney stepped from the darkness his cup hanging from his hand. "Was that himself?" He rubbed his eyes.

"Missed the Sons of Hibernia reunion!" Nolan wetted his handkerchief and clasped it to his eye. He remembered the two New Yorkers and motioned to Mahoney, "Gentlemen, a kin of yours I'm sure. Mahoney, Co B, 8-OVI. As Irish as shamrocks."

"A friend of the family of the Fourth — a good lot, but tempermental." Mahoney stretched out a hand. "I didn't want to interrupt your earlier debate."

Nolan winced and fixed an annoyed grimace as if to say, next time when punches are thrown feel free.

"Sure enough, Meagher of the Sword." Daniel rubbed his chin. Mahoney pulled a canteen from behind his shoulder, popped the cork on a ration of the elixir, and started filling cups in lieu of the peace pipe. The men emptied their coffee and accepted the whiskey, even at dawn it seemed a first-rate idea. Daniel nodded, "Not like himself to handle things so calmly."

In the spirit of Lenten penance, the three Ohioans bit their tongues while the Irishmen wore themselves out praising McClellan, Meagher and the Army of the Potomac. But when they had left, Mahoney put his head close to his comrades. "Can they be serious about that cigar store Indian?"

"You remember that crock back in West Virginia?" Nolan slipped his hand inside his shirt and struck a pose, "'Soldiers, I have heard that there was danger here. I have come to place myself at your head...to share it with you. But I fear that you will not find foemen worthy of your steel.' God! What shit!"

"Read well in the papers." Mahoney absently drew out a cigar to the absolute covetous stares of his two friends. He silenced all questions by pulling out two more and passed them around. "Just don't ask." The private bit off the butt and reached for a taper. "Merry Christmas, gentlemen, Compliments of...uh...General McClellan's orderly who folded three of a kind on a pair of fours."

XXIV

Only the gold fringe fluttered down the seams of emerald silk and when a slight breeze caught it, the flag rippled gently at its silver-mounted standard. The colors of the 69th New York flanked on either side by those of the 88th and 63rd New York guarded the entrance of the brigade commander's tent. These colors were legend in the Army. "They shall never retreat from the charge of lances."

The aide left Quinn outside and proceeded into the tent. The swarm of staff and orderlies paused over their papers and maps to eye the private with curiosity. It was rare for a mudsill to be summoned to headquarters to the satisfaction of the private. Officers beyond immediate family, i.e., company level, were religiously avoided.

The officer emerged and held open the flap, "The General will see you now." With his dispatches in his hand the aide passed around a labyrinth of tables and working officers, mounted his horse and rode off. Inside the General sat at a field desk reading a report, squinting at figures he did not like and made notations. He briefed it again, made another notation, put the pages together and set them aside. He picked up his cigar. He motioned Quinn to a camp stool.

The General looked probably forty — not old for a field commander, still trim and erect for a man of middle age. His eyes were piercing and turned cold when he saw something that displeased him. An imperial, a firm beard hid any flaws such as a weak mouth or chin.

Legend followed Meagher like a comet's tail. Not like the scandal-hunting General Daniel Sickles, who had shot his wife's lover in cold blood in the middle of Washington. It had been Stanton, the current Secretary of War, who had gotten the Congressman off on a defense of temporary insanity — the first such case to be successfully pleaded on that motion.

But all the same Meagher was an enigma. He had escaped exile in Tasmania to come to America. But behind were the graves of his wife and child. Meagher was not a bully or a hothead, he was educated, literate, and a speaker that could boil the blood of an expatriated Irishmen. Prison had not quelled the fire and zeal that glowed in the deep black eyes. No one questioned Meagher's ability to command.

The General gave the papers to another aide who had abruptly entered the tent. In a polished brogue, the Irish rebel whispered instructions that he was not to be disturbed. As he passed, the officer nodded at the private cordially. Taking a long draw on a cigar, Meagher turned a gentle light on the uncomfortable visitor, "Do you know who I am?"

"Yes, sir." Quinn replied automatically. "Brigadier General ..."

"None of that." Meagher brushed away the formalities like a puff of smoke, "That's not why I've asked you here."

Quinn waited and then whispered, "You are the last man to see my father alive."

"Yes," Even so Meagher was visibly shaken by the admission. "I guess I am. We spent the last night together, I was hardly your age. Your father was a tower of resolve, strong, but grieved that the cause had cost so much. Terrified for you. He was a brave man to the last. He hoped you would be."

A voice...smokey haze...the tenor strains of "Minstral Boy". Then the abyss of sleep and abandonment. "Yes, Sir, I always knew that. The Crown wouldn't hang any other."

"You're right there." Meagher sighed. "The Crown feared him and hanged him to stamp out his fire. But the fire burns on...the cause goes on..."

"Yes, Sir. In you."

"I'm just a small part of it. After this war is over, these regiments — Irish sons all — will return home to fight but we'll be trained and the match of the Black Watch and what ever black guards the German Princess can send against us. We will not be squelched so easily. We are lucky — you and I. `Two countries we love, and two mottoes we have And we'll join them as one, in the banner we bear.'"

"Sir?"

"That is why I asked you here."

"Sir?" Quinn saw what was coming but could not deflect it.

"You belong with us, Quinn. Your own kind. You belong with the 69th fighting under the Emerald colors. I can get you a transfer. You can be my personal aide. You have experience — West Virginia, the Valley — and the blood of your father in your veins. We will finish our work here and then the real enemy — the one that hanged your father and many good men beside him. You will take your father's place. Your homeland."

Quinn shook his head, "This is my homeland, Sir. It is what I know." He thought of his mother and his best and only friend. What would he tell them? "With all due respect, Sir, I am grateful for the honor. I do appreciate it. But, Sir, my rightful place is on the skirmish line with the Fourth, Sir. It's not that I couldn't be replaced, but I have earned that on my own."

Quinn ached. But what more was there to say? How he wanted to know his father...to put a face to the voice...to embrace him second hand. But his mother had baptized him with American dreams... Myra... a farm of his own without genuflecting at the knee. "You're Irish..." the General demanded.

"Begging your pardon, Sir. I'm American... Ohio... Union more to the point. This Union is my fight, Sir, the only one. And when it's done, I'm going home to get married, raise children, corn and beans and avoid anything so much as an argument." Quinn paused, "General you hear Irish fifes, I hear bugles and lullabies."

"You want this fight, Quinn?" Meagher challenged the revolutionary that must be in him down deep.

"No, Sir. It came and got me. Nolan, my friend, only one in fact I had back in Dublin, made me see for all our differences we are still a Union."

"Nolan Giles. St. Giles, patron saint of the abandoned. Ironic that? Not Brit?"

"No, Sir. Not that he will admit, Welsh on his mother's side. He says close enough to Irish but without the leprechauns."

"Don't believe in leprechauns." Meagher puffed a halo and smiled. He was enjoying himself. "Blasphemous."

"Sir. Maintains they are a figment of a mind pickled with too many legends and too much ale." The General smiled again and Quinn surprised him with one in return. The General saw his father — the same benevolence, the same quiet nobility in the face of death. It was the night he was taken away to die.

"Differences don't matter. Hell, begging the General's pardon, in West Virginia we fought with the Deutch and couldn't understand them half the time, and the West Virginians...them very little better. But we still got the job done. The purpose was the same--just as you said back at the fire. "

"This Dublin you cherish, it Irish?"

"Not a lick, Sir!"

"How'd they come by the name?"

"Wishful thinking I guess. Not much of a town even. Taverns and farms mostly."

Meagher digested it for awhile. "This friend of yours will probably get you killed. Any man who takes on a stevedore twice his size ain't got a lick of sense."

"Sounds Irish to me." Quinn winked, then added, "Nolan fights his own fights. He doesn't expect a friend to risk himself to save him from his own foolhardiness. But he knows we'll come. He said once, we're like wasps in a nest, challenge one and the lot lights on you. As long as the disagreement was between the two we would have kept our distance, but as soon as the other put in his two bits, well, it's a big regiment. Sir."

"How do you gain from this cause?"

"I don't think I believed in the cause when the war began. Never even thought much about the Union, it was just there. But Nolan, well, he had to get away from his Father. My mother was afraid... we... sometimes I think Nolan has had to be braver than all of us. He's never tasted the sweetness of life only the bitter. If he fights, I fight with him.

"Every time I'm called to the line I have to decide all over whether or not it's worth my life. At first I was afraid I didn't believe enough, there would come a day when I couldn't answer and I'd run. After awhile I don't have to ask anymore, I've gambled too much on it, and it's automatic. For Nolan it's shooting craps with no money. If he survives maybe God will pay up on an overdue debt."

Quinn accepted the General's offer of a whisky and Meagher nodded for him to go on, "Did you know my mother was pregnant when my father was hanged? I've got two brothers at home. I love them but Nolan's closer to me than either of them. Hell, every man in the company is closer to me than them."

The General nodded."I think your friend will survive if you come with us."

Quinn looked grieved, "I'm all he has. He don't know it yet but his father — never much as a family — was shot by a drunk. I guess it must be about a month ago. I just got the news in the last mail. Somehow I've got to tell him."

Quinn quenched the fire in his throat with the last of the glass. "Anyway, Sir, I guess I'll stay where I am. They ain't all Irish, but you wouldn't know the difference when they fight."

Meagher rose, "You have time to give it more thought, Son. We will be traveling together. If you ever need me...goes for your friend Nolan...my door is always open so to speak."

Quinn snapped to attention. "Thank you, Sir!"

Quinn made his way back to camp. "Some skirmishers you two make." He strode into the circle without either of his pards so much as raising an eyebrow. Either they were drunk or...Nolan ran his sleeve across his tear-stained face. "It's Mac."

"How's the little Scot?"

"He died." Nolan choked.

The cocky little Scot dead. Quinn recoiled. He was feeling drunk.

XXV

Bull Run! The Fourth pushed the advance of the long blue column guiding it down the Warrenton Turnpike on the double quick toward Manassas Junction. It was the eleventh hour salvation for Major-General John Pope and his 75,000 men of the Army of Virginia who had met disaster on the Orange and Alexandria Railroad. There the wiley strategist Robert Lee and his nearly barefoot Army of Northern Virginia had checkmated Pope's superior numbers.

McClellan's troops trailed back the twenty miles to Alexandria. They had been slow in coming but once they were set in motion they came on fast. The veterans urged the column at a pace that even they found excruciating in the heat and dust of late August. Lungs pounded against their ribs like hammers, the lips cracked and bled from the dust and salt. The faces and uniforms were ghost-like — salted with the fine dust that churned up in clouds pulverized under their feet.

And they came on offering no quarter for their own who staggered away from the column onto the side of the road to collapse with heat stroke and fatigue. It was no safer there. If the ambulances and wagons did not rescue them quickly or they could not scramble out of the way, they were trampled under by the retreat.

The column cleared the road only for the cannon coursing to the front, gunners, mounted on lathered teams. The narrow road was congested with three columns, the center racing to the front, and one on either side, the retreat flowing to the rear. They were moving away from the battle. There was none of the great hurrah on their lips. They spit venom at the upcoming troops, "Could have beaten 'em if you were only up, Yank."

"Sunshine boys. There's a real fight up ahead."

"Carry me back to old west Virginny where life was easy and plenty for dinny."

"Got a real war ahead, Plow Boy! Bring your gun?"

File closers herded the brigade ahead. At the last minute McClellan had been ordered by Washington to move part of his army north to assist Pope. The Indian fighter had collided with Lee on nearly the same site that Lieutenant-General Joseph Johnston had defeated Irvin McDowell's Federals a year earlier. Not much had changed in a year, the outcome had been mostly the same. Only the cast of characters had changed.

Pope, reinforced with three corps, had planned to ensnair Jackson and then Longstreet. But the Virginian would not be caught; he struck Pope at Groveton at dusk on August 28. The next day Pope renewed the attack but his assault was badly coordinated. The butternut Confederates held on until Longstreet came up to hammer the Federals against Stonewall's anvil. Just as Pope fell back his right and left flanks crushed, McClellan's reinforcements arrived.

The Turnpike dead-ended into balloons of smoke that drifted above the trees. The roll of cannon and the staccato of musket fire were waning. Bugles were calling retreat. The forces were pulling away from each other. The column would be too late.

Kendrick cursed Nolan who ran all the faster like a bloodhound to the fox. From porches and fence rails Virginia farmers waved fists at the river of blue that passed, "That's right, keep running, your judgment's ahead. Jackson is going to give it to ya. Keep running, Yank, straight to perdition."

From the safety of the windows, Southern women chortled, "There they go like moths to the fire. The son of Light Horse Harry is up there, you'll get yours."

The Fourth had endured it all only to arrive in time for another rear guard action — protecting the backs of the retreating army.

As a final curtain, the skies salted with the sulphur nitrate from the cannons opened up. Rain washed sweat and grime into the eyes of the marching soldiers. Blood from the ambulance wagons washed into the dust. Wounded moved in open, springless wagons that jolted and bumped over rocks and ruts. Some cursed, others prayed for relief, others asked to be shot. Rain washed the salt and black powder into their wounds. Aside from a canteen from a passing samaritan the rain was the only water they would receive until Alexandria.

The Brigade moved into line to hold back the Confederates while the Army could get away. The hollow-eyed defeated continued to pass. "Mac's boys, always a day late and a dollar short." And the same old refrain, "Damned Westerners, if you had kept Jackson in the Valley..."

General Kimball reined up. He did not bolt up in his stirrups, windmill his saber above his head to rouse his men to the front. They would have loved to hear the words, "Advance! Ohio, by file into line. Take those bastards and we'll show these boys how to fight." Instead he ordered his officers to deploy the men to guard the retreat. Bull Run was not their defeat. Only a defeat that they could not prevent.

XXVI

The evangelist strode to the center of the assembled. The icy winds of the Rappahannock coursed under the ridges of the tent and tugged at his black, swallow-tailed coat. He seemed an immense crow wading into a sea of Saxon-blue great coats and dark forage caps. In spite of the cold, he was bareheaded, his white hair clipped tight to his head like a helmet. His clean-shaven face was the color and sheen of faded pink silk; his large white hands clasped a worn-black Bible in front of him. The preacher composed himself and raised his eyes toward heaven. Then he bowed and closed them, his lips moving silently.

This was a small chapter in the Great Awakening coursing through the Armies. Men with their backs to the enemy were turning their faces to Christ in ever increasing numbers. Religious tracts were handed out by the Christian Commission along with the other necessities of survival. The officers enjoyed the benefit, a sober God-fearing soldier was easier to handle. From top down these revivals had the blessing of the commanders even if they did not partake themselves.

The overture of coughing tugged at his concentration. Occasionally the evangelist opened his eyes, cast an accusing glare at an irreverent distraction and then as if he were drifting off to sleep, close them again. The lines tightened around his forehead and his lips pursed as his prayers grew to a climax. He threw his head back and his eyes were wide coals staring black and cold into the assembled. The body seemed on the verge of levitation. He surveyed them silently. The coughs and whispers faded, then evaporated until there was only the wind howling through the tent like a great pipe organ.

"I went today to buy a Testament..." he began so softly

that his little congregation bent forward in spite of themselves. "Yes I went to Mr. Bullock's wagon to buy a Testament for a troubled soldier agonizing over the state of his soul. He is one of yours and he lies racked with shivers and fire, calling for his God to come and take him out of that miserable body." The preacher drew out the vowels and pulled at the words like taffy. "Is it his soul crying out? Is it unquiet about its judgment before its maker? Is it wrestling with the sin that will keep it from soaring to its heavenly reward?

"I went to Mr. Bullock's wagon. He purveys in all things for the revival of the body and the appeasement of appetites. There are slabs of cured pork, cans of milk and peaches, tent halves, shirts, soap, matches to strike a fire to cook a meal and warm the aching bones against the dampness of these interminable winter nights.

"All these Mr. Bullock had in gaudy supply, Gentlemen, but he did not have a Testament for my tormented friend. He did not have the medicine to soothe the wasted faith of a dying cavalier. His soul will have to find its way to heaven without the map of salvation!"

A long black arm catapulted the black Testament overhead like a shooting star and held it there. Some of the soldiers were transfixed as if they had never seen the black book before. Others took up a new chorus of coughs to relieve their discomfort. And a few stared accusingly at the perimeter of sergeants and officers who kept them prisoner of the itinerant savior. They would be there for the duration. The cynical and the bored huddled down into their capes and went to sleep.

"Soldiers, do you go into battle unarmed — with nothing to fight your enemy but your fists? No! I see each of you with a cartridge box and a bayonet sheathed at your waist. Before your tents are stacked rifles. Beyond the tents are acres of cannon and enough shell to tear this earth asunder and kill the enemy ten times over.

"Yet, the greatest enemy of all, the heathen spirit of Satan, is allowed — no, invited — to walk among you, and you go unarmed against him. I have seen his bible in your hands — the playing cards, the flasks that you pass among you, the novels that load down your pockets. But do you have a Testament to pass to a friend to quench his thirsty soul? A Book of Common Prayer to console his mind? A tract to enlighten his confused faith?"

Reverend Collin George charged down the aisle between two companies, with the Testament waving above him like the colors. Soldiers leaned out of his way and then turned to watch him pass. Some faces were dark with confusion, others red with rage, still others bored. George stopped dead as if by inspiration pointing a finger only inches away from the face of Newby Monroe, "Do you have a Testament, Son, to nourish your soul?" Newby froze like a cornered animal. He did not move his head right or left, up or down.

"A soldier without his Testament is as unarmed before the Judgment seat of the Almighty as if he had gone into the face of the enemy without a weapon. He does not carry it for protection. He does not carry it as witness to his salvation. It is not his ticket into heaven. It is his sign of witness, of accepting God as his Savior! Do you believe!"

Reverand George pivoted on his heels, looking for a new victim, he shouted, "The believer carries it to nourish his soul. It is like a flaming sword before the serpent."

Nothing! There should be some fire. But these troops were like stone. The Evangelist scanned the congregation searching the steel faces of the veterans for some sign that his message had fallen on fertile ground somewhere. Find the leader, break him down, get him to crave baptism and the rest will follow. Anonymous they huddled like a flock of jays in the snow.

The blonde one...there. He seethed contempt. If he breaks...George waded over the men, until he towered above the corporal. "Are you ready to meet your salvation, Soldier?" He trumpeted like a bugle, then thrust a finger into Nolan's face like a bayonet. "Do you have your Testament, Soldier? Show it to me? Give witness before all here assembled that you have taken the Lord Jesus Christ as your Lord and Savior." If he raised it up the soldier showed solidarity with the message of the Evangelist. If not, he admitted defeat and damnation. George had him either way.

Nothing. No response of any kind. "Are you the Christian to lead these men on their righteous crusade against the heathen slave masters?"

Nothing. Nolan did not flinch. He did not cowar, look up, or even blink. Not a breath. The Corporal kept eyes forward as if at attention.

From the perimeter Chase braced ready for trouble. He did not like the signs. "Don't provoke that one." Chase breathed. Lieutenant Jones nodded and set himself to move into the group at first sign of trouble.

Wouldn't the old coot be surprised. Nolan restrained a smile. His mother's Bible nestled in his breast pocket as close to him as his own heart. Its pages were matted together, water stained and wrinkled. But he did not reach for it. Instead he sat rigid, immovable as a wall against the force that bore down on him again. "Son, I charge you, admit your sinfulness to the joy of God and all of us assembled!" George howled like the wind.

"No!" Nolan hissed. He was done with accusations,

with threats of damnation by preachers who set themselves up as judges of who was good and who was evil. He would not be George's sacrificial lamb.

Giles raised his eyes slowly and fixed them on the Evangelist with the cold contempt of a hunter just before pulling the trigger. George held his ground, but the brimstone was fading out of him. He bent into Nolan's face.

There was the unmistakable whisper of whisky on the preacher's breath. It filled Giles's nostrils and nearly made him vomit. "Do you mock your Creator with your arrogance? Or do you mock His messenger?" George hissed acid. "You are dammed if you are not born again! Dammed to Satan's pit of no return! Dammed by the hand of Almighty God! Dammed if you die without baptism! Dammed if you do not believe and raise your voice up with the heavenly hosts. Otherwise you will be lost for all eternity, broken and cast away into the fires of hell.

"Before the lamb who was crucified, we must prostrate ourselves before the Lord to be one with the clay in which he molded us." George molded his hand into a fist and thrust it at Quinn. "See it, Soldier. Flesh of the flesh begat down from Adam, molded from the clay of Eden. It is the stuff of what you were made and what you lost through the sin of Eve. It is fresh, pink and alive for a short time. Today, tomorrow, or years from now it will mix again with the land from where it came, when you are lowered into your grave. We are a fleeting moment on the earth conjured from nothing more than this."

The Catholic Irishman had been tried and convicted of worse by other men speaking for God. He let the words roll over him like a breeze no more no less than the insults and jeers from the tavern drunks.

George moved down to the next man in the line, and

the preacher rammed his fist to within an inch of his nose. Christie smacked it away. A reaction! At last the Evangelist had his victim. He gripped the soldier's hand and pressed the fist into his own palm and molded the fingers around it. "We are the same, Boy, called from the void. Damp, primeval, like your soul, it languishes without purpose, life, calling. Clasp my hand, Boy. Take the outstretched hand of God." George opened the fingers and extended his hand around the boy's palm.

"Feel salvation, Boy! Feel it! Feel down to the depths of your ragged soul. Feel the emptiness, feel the uselessness, feel the cold darkness of the death...it's death that claims us all — on the battlefield, in the coughing expiration of a hospital, or in the cold, loneliness of our beds as it steals over us like a shadow."

"I killed a man!" Christie whispered.

"What?" the Inquisitor recoiled.

Nolan wanted to stand up and with one blow blast the man into the river. Instead, he put a hand on his friend's shoulder. As Christie's tear-stained face turned, Nolan shook his head. Christie drew himself up and wrestled control. His eyes grew hard and fixed.

The moment had escaped.

George moved from man to man, eager to make quota. "My Poor Souls!" He thundered, his fist piercing the air as if Satan sparred before him, "Death awaits. It will most certainly claim us — clean or unclean. No man knows the time and the place. The saved will be gathered up like leaven bread, the damned plunge into hell fire. "

"Amen... Amen... Hear the Lord!" A soldier too long away from home, too cold, too hungry. His pard dead on the march from consumption.

Nolan hated the evangelist for breaking the brave boy

down. The Evangelist had his soul at last, others would come. He raced to him extending his Bible over the heads of two rows of men, "Behold the Word. Pray for the forgiveness, My Sons! Pray for the lifesaving water of baptism that springs from the Savior like a fountain. Come with me to the river to be baptized. Baptized and wash your black soul in the Jordan of salvation before it is too late. Before you walk into the valley of death, wash away your sins..."

"Amen!" the soldier wailed on cue.

"Amen, I say to you. Come to Zion! Come to the River! Wash and sing the great Amen! Raise your voices to the heavens, Amen! Amen, my Sons! God blesses the soil which drinks in the water."

"Amen!" The soldier rose to his knees, "Amen!"

"Let us go to the river!" Only five gathered behind their comrade. Giles watched them go. The rest were dismissed. Nolan walked out of the tent a free man. From beneath his great coat he pulled out a flask against the cold and was about to drink. The bottle froze in mid air as Father Corby, chaplain of the Irish Brigade, stared it down. The rugged man was leaning against a bare oak, his eyes stone behind the full, black beard.

As if bidden, Quinn and Giles strode up to the Irish Priest who had left the lecture halls of Fordham University for the ministry of the battle field. Giles had liked him immediately, hearing him preach gently, consoling his men in their grief, sustaining them in their fear, tending their needs, administering last sacraments on the battlefield as the bullets thudded into the ground around him.

"Well, Father, do you think it will stick?" Giles looked after the small fold, collecting by the frozen river. He was relieved that they were not being dunked. The Evangelist had some sense.

"Well," the Priest folded his arms in front of him, "He got a good house. Say that for him. It'd consent to be baptized in a religion he's selling if it kept the boys on the righteous side between Sundays. What about you, Giles, not going to be baptized?" The Priest winked.

"My father was a preacher in the same fashion as Cotton Mather here." He pulled the thin, faded leather volume from his pocket, "Pardon me, Father, but I have sinned."

The Chaplain winked and Nolan caressed the cover. "I bet there are a thousand more of these in one form or another, nestled in the blankets and pockets of the Rebs across the river. They will read them when there is light enough and draw from the verses the blessed right and privilege to lift his rifle and shoot me dead.

"Over hear we get the same interpretation. That our cause is sanctified. God is a Union man. Either way men need God to take the responsibility for what they do. `It's all in God's hands they say."

The priest reached to comfort the boy, but Giles recoiled as if a hand had been raised against his cheek. "Sorry." Nolan looked away. "I probably should be down there by the river. But there isn't enough water to wash away all my transgressions. I'll keep them awhile longer, I would be nothing without them. They make me want to live. Nothing like a clean soul to make a man give up and lay down a martyr."

Giles liked the priest. Corby was not full of bluster like the Jesuit Father Dillon who had been known to walk through the camp of the New York brigades kicking breakfast plates into the fires and throwing dirt into cups of coffee just because a soldier slept through services. Father Corby pulled on his chasuble after morning inspection, calling the boys together and blessing them all, generals and privates, protestants and catholics.

The priest was reluctant to let the boy go," God chooses His own from the most unlikely in a flock."

Nolan threw an arm around his pard's shoulders and jostled him, "Well, I have Quinn here. He's one of your lambs, Father, duly baptized, enrolled and sealed right down to his emerald green soul. But will do time for his cursing. I plan to get into heaven on his coat tails."

Giles extended a hand, "Thanks for the sentiments, Father. We're due on picket." As the unrequited lamb and his conscience turned toward their tents, the Irish confessor lifted his hand in blessing to follow them. "In Nominae Patri...

XXVII

It had been reasonable marching weather when the II Corps left Warrenton on the fifteenth of November, 1862. The wing of Sumner's Grand Division constituted almost one-third of the Army of the Potomac, and made the forty miles to Falmouth in two days of fast marching. Chase had been right. A veteran marched from habit. At the order, a man's legs stepped off; at the order they halted. In between they turned over on their own, leaving his mind to its own devices. Nolan pulled the visor down to the bridge of his nose, dropped his eyelids to mere slits and guided off the heels of the soldier in front.

They had traveled this road before. Last May when they had left the Shenandoah Valley with a sure foot toward Richmond. But it had turned out to be Falmouth, a Grand Review for the President, Stanton, and McDowell. Instead of going on south "Shield's Light-Horse Cavalry" hightailed the hundred miles back to the Shenandoah to fight Jackson, which was what they had been doing before being called East.

Before the "bungle-brained" wild-goose chase, Companies B and C had made themselves something of heroes. It had been wonderful! They had just marched over the Blue Ridge in time to see the enemy fleeing out the back door of Front Royal. The Rebs had fired the town. The two Companies leading the regiments at the double quick made straight for the supply yards. Without regard for their own lives, men charged into the burning boxcars to save what they could. Already the heat had ignited the ammunition cases and a deadly crack of flying projectiles pinged against the studs like popcorn. Powder hissed and the flames burned black enough to disorient anyone in the inferno. Quinn had called his friend's name from the door and Nolan made for the sound of the voice, a crate of Springfields burning blisters into his hands. The troops had saved the precious supplies, the rolling stock and the locomotives. The rest of the brigade saved the depot buildings and warehouses, Jackson's bonfire destroyed little.

The first year of the war had been spirited. Romney, PawPaw, Bloomery Gap, then the Shenandoah Valley. McDowell, New Market, Luray. The apple-blossoms blooming in the orchards of Woodstock, the adventure of Weyer's Caves up the valley, of catching the Rebels bathing in Stoney Creek and watching them skedaddle to the tune of .58 caliber shot whizzing over their heads.

Then there was the loss of Colonel Andrews, and the hard-swearing Colonel Lander, who hated Secech in inverse proportion to the love he felt for his men. Of Sam Johns and Jamie MacGowan and the others who no longer answered the long roll.

Nolan had been thinking on it as he turned the bend in the Turnpike and there on the bank the man stood as solid and immovable as a statue. His staff surrounded him like bridesmaids. Major-General Ambrose Burnside astride his horse, enveloped in his great coat salted with the rain and snow. The crown of his black slouch hat rose like a mountain above an expanse of brim that shadowed all but the thick growth of sideburns for which he was famous. He watched the Army of the Potomac — McClellan's army — move past.

Now it was his, and he was marching with all possible speed southeast toward Falmouth to establish a base of supply from the railroad to Aquia on the Potomac. Then he would march across the Rappahannock on pontoon bridges to Fredericksburg and on to Richmond. Like other generals before him, Burnside saw Richmond as the life-giving waters of the Confederacy. However, there was nothing magical about the city. Except for the business of government and the Tredegar Iron Works, the capital was an asylum for old men, women, and children. Why he had chosen the harder way when there were easier routes was hard to guess.

Lincoln had pinned his hopes on a man who had no right to think that luck would strike him after thirty-eight years of near misses. Ambrose Burnside, West Point Class of 1847, bad at poker and jilted at the altar. When his classmates were earning brevets, he was stranded at garrison duty in the Mexican War. Later he was wounded by the Apaches. He had invented a carbine, but went bankrupt trying to get it produced. Sold the patent to a firm who made a fortune on it without sharing a dime with the inventor. His friend McClellan saved the man from bankruptcy by giving him a job with the Illinois Central Railroad. With the war his friend brought him up through the ranks to command the IX Corps. But their friendship had fallen on hard times and Antietam had brought it to the breaking point. Burnside had been stymied at the Rohrback Bridge. By the time he got his men across, Powell Hill was up with the last of Jackson's men. The bloodiest day of the war ended in stalemate. McClellan was soon relieved and Burnside given command over even his own objections.

"Well, he looks like a general." Quinn wiped his eyes against the November rain.

"You can paint a cow plop orange but it don't make it pumpkin pie." Nolan spit.

"I had a hound at home looked just like that," Christie snickered. Nolan rewarded that crack with a twist of tobacco. Kendrick marched silently alongside but said nothing.

"You boys could do with a healthy dose of respect."

Chase moved astride and reached for a share of the plug. He pulled off a portion and shared it with Kendrick.

As his troops passed, the General was more on view than the opposite. The Irish Brigade, ever loyal to McClellan had not taken the change of command gracefully and talked about mutiny. But Brigadier-General Winfield Scott Hancock had kept the powder keg of discontent under control. He had inherited them along with the rest of the First Divison upon the death of their old commander at Antietam. Hancock was more than enough for the job. The General didn't flinch under fire, had a sharp eye for the advantage, was a direct actionist and was reputed — that even though profanity was expressly forbidden by Army regulations — as pre-eminent above officers, men and mule drivers for the magnitude and sheer thunder of his profanity.

In spite of rain, rations the men cursed as "execrable", stubborn mules who sat back in the bottomless mud, stalled wagons, cranky officers, snow and rain in alternation, the morale of the Army was still good. But in the Fourth Ohio it was bad. Out of the original thousand men commissioned back in May of 1861, only one hundred ninety-six officers and men were present for duty when called to the line back at Warrenton. Most of the regiment was still back at Camp Ohio near Washington; some dying by inches with typhus, others in the fever sweats and cold seizures of dysentary. The regiment had been too sick to march to Antietam and the tenderfoot 132nd Pennsylvania had taken their place in the Brigade.

The 132nd now marched at the tail of the Divison not to slow the veterans down. Lieutenant-Colonel Charles Albricht having enough of their sloppy march, thought cadence would move them along in better order. He rode up to the boy who carried the large drum in front of his chest and bid him to beat it. But the boy, eyes forward, either did not hear or ignored the request. The Colonel bent lower and repeated the order a little louder this time. The boy shuffled along without even giving the slightest indication of the Colonel's existence. Albricht leaned over his horse to speak directly into the boy's ear and ordered him by all that was holy to beat the infernal drum or suffer the consequences of insubordination. Still the boy declined.

The Colonel reddened at the private's impudence. In the niche of time, a junior officer reined up by the commander and whispered, "Sir, there is a chicken in the drum."

Albricht shot up straight in the saddle and bellowed, "Well, why didn't you tell me the boy was sick. Take him to the rear and we'll deal with the situation later."

Sumner's troops reached Falmouth on the north bank of the Rappahannock on November 17. Nolan liked the neat rows of houses and shops of Frederickbrug on the opposite shore. But no traffic passed up the streets and no lights came from the windows at night. The town was deserted. Burnside could have taken the town without so much as a shot. But the General did nothing. A couple of hungry battalions would have been glad to storm the town just for something to do. Then troops could move into the warehouses and buildings to get out of the weather. But still no order came. Soldiers left idle out in the snow and rain rust.

The rest of the army came up 120,000 of them in all to camp in the open. Fires burned along Stafford Heights like a conflagration. They shimmered in a blanket down the ridge by the Lacy Mansion and east toward George Washington's boyhood home of Ferry Farm.

The token force of Confederates in Fredericksburg grew unmolested. Every day a soldier could tell by counting the flags who and how many had come up. The Yanks knew the enemy's banners as well as they knew their own.

Longstreet was up from Culpepper by the twenty-first. They camped south of the town on Marye's Heights the battleflags of McLaws, George Pickett, Low Armistead, Jimmy Kemper fluttered against the snow. Further east A.P. Hill and then D.H. Hill, Jackson's brother-in-law, and Jeb Stuart's cavalry guarded the extreme flank.

By mid-December the void behind Fredericksburg was a galaxy of campfires against the black winter nights. Nolan tallied the estimates he had read in papers. Longstreet had about 40,000, Jackson with Ewell's Division not quite that many, and Stuart's Cavalry about 10,000. That was ninety thousand men — give or take a battalion — camped on the high ground across the river.

There was the dull ache that opportunity had passed and in its place was a trap. Between the Union and Confederate forces was the town and the River. If the Union attacked they would have to lay bridges, and march through the town now ripe with sharpshooters. Those who survived continued up the open ground beyond into the face of the enemy without cover. There was going to be hell to pay.

Giles saw it. Every man down to the youngest drummer boy had only to look across the river to see his fate if the order came. They talked of nothing else as they cooked their coffee, shuddered in the wind, and cursed the red beef and tack. Suicide.

It all coalesced into a rage. Hot shakes throttled Nolan's whole body. The glittering flames beyond blurred into one great inferno. Over there the Rebels were nourishing themselves on Union coffee, telling stories, reading letters from home, and preparing for battle. Tomorrow or the day after he was going to die — not just killed by a Confederate shell or ball — but murdered by the arrogance of a shuck-headed general who didn't have the sense to count campfires. The General would live to resign, but Nolan would be dead. Quinn would be dead, Christie, Kendrick, all of them, who had survived to this point by their pluck and smarts — all for nothing. When the long roll sounded, a soldier stepped to the line and did not ask why or where.

"That fool has no more sense about war than a mule." Nolan growled.

"What?" Quinn inched from the cover. It was another half hour before he would relieve his friend on the picket line and he had been warming himself in the bushes.

"Up there!" Nolan nodded behind the white glazed river. Quinn didn't have to look, he had done his own counting.

Disaster was in the wind. Campfires flickered on opened Bibles, rosary beads filtered between the fingers of the Irish. Playing cards drifted on the little channels of water through pockets of ice. Profanity was mute. Bristling sergeants lost their bite. Quinn and others with family wrote careful letters filled at the heart with goodbyes, instructions for family businesses that should carry on in their absence. Some were even baptized.

XXVIII

The surgeons readied for the battle to save lives with as much tenacity as commanders planned for the assault in which they were taken. The ornate furniture of the Lacy House, the Georgian mansion that had entertained Washington and the Lees, was passed up to the attic to make room for litters. Doors were unhinged and laid across chairs as operating tables. Books were cleared from the shelves so casualties would be set one on top of another in their place. Heirloom rugs were rolled up before they were soaked with blood. Doctors opened medical chests, set out the ether, the chloroform, whiskey, and the morphine. Aside from the few rooms General Sumner used as his headquarters, the house would be the hub of the Medical Service. Brigade and regimental "hospitals" moved to any shelter from houses to barns.

Dr. Jonathan Letterman, Medical Director of the Army of the Potomac, was barking orders to his ambulance teams with the relentlessness of a drill sergeant. By the hour he worked them, refining the most efficient, gentle means of removing wounded from the field. He planned to send these teams out even before the bullets had stopped flying and meant to keep them at it until every wounded man was withdrawn. The doctor had fired the band members, laggards, ne'er do wells who the commanders had volunteered because they were useless on the firing line. Instead Letterman chose only men of quality and endurance from each company as carriers and drivers.

Throughout the afternoon, troops could hear the young surgeon barking at his teams, running to adjust a litter, demonstrating a more benevolent method of transporting a tender casualty, setting up entrance and exiting systems so teams did not lose valuabale time in traffic jams. The December freeze would not be forgiving — men would die quickly without immediate rescue.

White and brown habits fluttered in and out of the mansion. Religious orders of nuns had brought their nursing skills to the battle fields. And there was the phantom of the school teacher from Oxford, Massachusetts, Clara Barton who came with wagon-loads of lanterns, bandages, soup, tobacco, and the necessities as well as comforts to the troops.

Until the long roll reverberated, soldiers settled into camp life. They cleared back the woods to give them room for camps, depots of supplies, and grazing for horses and cattle. They gathered the wood for camp fires, earthworks, and huts or shebangs. Streets of these queer shelters with log sides and roofs of tent halves overlaid with pine boughs turned into cities. Most slept four men in relative comfort compared to tents in December. They offered such ammenities as racks of bed steads, stools and tables fashioned out of ration barrels. Many boasted of stoves and chimneys also of stacked ration barrels. The camp was as safe as a tinder box. Chimneys caught fire regularly and if the neighborhood "volunteer fire department" was not energetic enough flames spread to the roof and then from roof to roof.

Duty was brutal, but a soldier with time on his hands grumbled about the ache in his stomach, the state of the rations, the dirt, cold, and what family might be doing back home. Some malcontents still huddled over camp fires plotting the return of McClellan. Others watched the enemy come up and wondered what transpired behind the windows of the elegant plantation houses where generals conspired.

It was the second winter of the war for General Kimball's Brigade, but the first for many of Burnside's Eastern regiments. It was growing clear, the western and eastern troops might fight side by side, but they would not merge into a seamless fabric. In the ranks of the Fourth it was understood to a man — officer and enlisted alike — that any of their number putting on Eastern airs — "acting white" as they called it, would be summarily dealt with by a committee who would engage them in a "discussion" on the subject in some secluded spot.

The General rarely rode among his troops. McClellan had relished it and did so at every opportunity, to the delight of the men. "Hello, General!" "Give 'em hell, General!" "When are we going after 'em, General?"

But Burnside seldom went out except for Grand Reviews and there was none of the hail-fellow-well-met when he did. The General shook his head. Too much. He had told the President that he was not up to it. But Lincoln would not listen. Did not even give him a choice.

The Commander looked out from the second story window at the ninety thousand effectives down there. Should be able to sweep Satan out of hell with that number. But uncertainty ached like a dull pain in the back of his mind. A lion can lead lambs to victory, but a lamb can never lead lions. Something like that. What was he?

"What are they doing over there?" The Commander pointed through the translucent mist vaporized on the window.

Colonel John Parke put down his pen and walked to the window to look where Burnside pointed. At intervals men raced around a hollow square. The Chief of Staff turned to his commander, "Baseball, General. Those are some of General Doubleday's boys and I think the other team is...Ohio boys...the Fourth I think. Must be, those pirates are camped just over there."

The aide turned away, "Men are quite fond of it,

although the winter snows have added an unfortunate consequence to the game."

"What's that?"

"Casualties." Parke nodded. "They have a tendency to erupt into a fury of snowballs. Casualties enough for a surgeon's attention."

Burnside nodded and the officer returned to his papers. He should have known that. It was obvious from Parke's tone he thought so too.

Where are those pontoons? Another government snafu. They should have been here a month ago. Damned those bureaucrats! We could have been across the river and on our way to Richmond. Time. He who hesitates... McClellan hesitated. He must not show himself another laggard. Time! The greatest enemy of all. Jackson had come up. Lee would be getting ready, digging rifle pits, placing cannon. But with Three Grand Divisions and Hunt's cannon he still should be able to execute his plan. Hit them on the flank, surround them, and shove them out of the way. Yes, the plan would still work. He must have those pontoons!

At the briefing, his generals had insisted. The plan was now obsolete. Their advantage of numbers was canceled out by the enemy's possession of the high ground. But the numbers were vast, three Grand Divisions. He went over it again in his mind. They would attack on two flanks — a battle front four miles wide. Hit them hard on the left at Hamilton's Crossing with Franklin's Left Grand Division — Hooker's Middle Division in reserve. He would sweep them and come around and hit Lee from behind. Then Sumner's and Hooker's Grand Divisions would go in from the front and right of Marye's Heights and Lee would be crushed between the two. He had gone over it time and again in his head. It was sound.

Hancock, damned insubordinate for a brigadier, had objected almost before the words were out of his mouth. Burnside restrained a smile. At Antietam McClellan gave Hancock command of the dead Israel Richard's Division. Got Meagher's bloody Irish in the bargain. That will take some of the starch out of those elegant, pristine collars of his.

Hancock set upon him like an upperclassman, his voice edged to the very point of insubordination. He ran his finger across the map tracing the Confederate lines. "Sir, the Confederates have the high ground all along here, from water line to water line — the Rappahannock on the right to Massoponax Creek on the left. Stuart's Cavalry guards the lower flank. Solid! Prime ground, an artilleryman's dream. Alexander will blot us out before we are out in the open. Lee can move troops almost at leisure, concentrate them down on us in converging fire while our boys march straight up this shelf without any cover at all. Straight out in the open.

"Water's on their side, our enemy! We'll be slowed by the canal and the ditch and the river will be at our backs. There are only two small bridges over that ditch and the Confederates will take care of those with the first salvos. The men will have to cross the ditches nearly single file, Sir, under fire... They will be cut down before they can reform."

Hancock had been a McClellan man — hell, they all were — Meade, Reynolds. Except Hooker. Hooker's allegiances were to Hooker. Burnside swallowed hard.

"I am fully aware of their position, General." Burnside reproached. "But by the time you are ordered into action, General Franklin will have attacked with the First, Sixth, Eleventh, and Twelfth Corps, Lee's Army will be chaos. That's about 30,000 men, General, more than enough. Hell, by that time most of the work should be done, Lee on the retreat and your work will be largely in support."

The commanders exchanged worried glances. They knew that Burnside had not sent out Averell and his Cavalry to reconnoiter the Southern position. If he had he would know how many men were hidden behind Marye's Heights. The other division commanders knew of the value of doing their homework. Each had sent out his own detachments — even walked the Union lines himself every night to keep abreast of the Confederate movements.

Reynolds put a hand on Hancock's shoulder and the general relaxed. But Hancock's mind was on more than Confederate entrenchments and batteries. The Confederate commanders were men he knew. Friends from a long career in the service going back nearly twenty years to the Academy. Armisted and Harry Heath, Jackson, Pickett and Longstreet. These men knew how to ring the best out of what they had. Put them at a disadvantage of guns and equipment and they made up for it in surprise, nerve and spunk. Give them the advantage of ground and they would kill you.

In Los Angeles Major Armisted had been Hancock's senior. When the war broke out the North Carolinian followed the course of his native state. Before leaving he made a gift to the young captain of his uniforms. But Hancock would not need them. In a rare move of brilliance McClellan had jumped Hancock three grades to brigadier and the General had proved himself worthy since.

Burnside looked up to these men, the impeccably-attired Hancock, John Reynolds, who had been commandant at West Point before the war, the thorny Darius Couch commanding the II Corps, the righteous O.O. Howard. Burnside's old Corps was now under Wilcox, the V Corps under Butterfield who loved music. And shifting on tired legs was the aging William French, whose division included

Nathan Kimball and those troops from Ohio and West Virginia that had beaten Lee and Jackson in the West. There was Sturgis, who had fought the Indians and whose pluck and shrewdness had saved his force from being stampeded by buffalo. Another Indian fighter John Buford of Kentucky, and the artillery genius Henry Hunt.

How he wished he had the trust of such men. But they would follow orders because they had to, and their men would follow them in turn. If he could not have their confidence, duty would have to be enough.

"Sir!" an aide broke through the door. "The pontoons are here." Burnside raised a hand in salute to fate. "Very good, Captain, Notify the engineers and put Lieutenant Comstock to work immediately. The orders are still the same, six bridges — three up three down. He knows what to do."

In an army where confusion and inertia were the rules of the day, Lieutenant Comstock was a marvel. He had the talent for writing clear, concise instructions and a procedure for everything. He drilled his engineers so even the most routine task was done by the numbers with snap and polish. Below the Lacy Mansion two bridges would go across with one more further south at the railroad. Three more down river near Deep Run and the Landsowne Valley Road. Baggage was ordered to the rear. Troops began to cook up rations, and stock their cartridge belts.

As meat fried around ramrods and coffee boiled, many bent over paper braced against rifle stocks to write what could be their last letter home. Others saw to the business of making sure that they would not be numbered among the casualties listed as "Unknown". On the backs of playing cards or letters, men with premonitions penciled their names and regiments and pinned them to the inside of their great coats.

Just below the Lacy House, flat-bottomed boats were brought down to the bank. The Engineers would unload and lash one to another until they extended into two swaying bridges wide enough for artillery and men to cross. That is, if all went well.

But it went badly from the start. As the engineers bent to the work, General Barksdale's Mississippians hidden in warehouses that backed onto the river bank began shooting from windows and doorways. Companies dropped into the black water. The fire was so hot the Federals retreated leaving dead and dying on the scaffolding.

Each time the unarmed engineers exposed themselves to the work Confederate sharpshooters picked them off with alarming accuracy — a groan, and then the crack of ice collpasing under a man's weight, and then nothing. From the bank Union infantry opened fire to no advantage, the sharpshooters were well covered.

Brigadier General Henry Hunt rolled thirty-six cannon into position on the riverbank and blazed away at close range. Engineers moved out again under the umbrella of shell. As if they were immune to cannonshot, the Confederates reappeared to fire again.

Work was going badly. By noon the next day the Chief of Artillery had lost his patience and ordered up one hundred forty-seven cannon into position. Everything in his artillery depot from ten pounder Parrotts to four-and-a-half-inch siege guns blazed fifty rounds each directly into the town. Shells ignited plumes of black smoke and red fire balls. Grand old homes that had stood since the Revolution were splinters and charcoal. The Mississippians dropped back.

Nolan and Quinn watched the cannonading from their position above stafford heights. Winter gusts drifted the gray sulphur smoke back across the river to settle into an eeriness around them. They walked on clouds. Nolan felt light headed and giddy. It was if the battle were already over and his soul had risen from his frozen corpse. "I am going to die!"

The windows of the Phillips' House were slate in the opaque dim of evening. Burnside was in there, probably just sitting down to dinner. "If I shot the Son of a Bitch now the worst they could do is shoot me. What's the difference of us two, to save thousands? I am going to die anyhow."

"What are you mumbling about? You sounding mighty queer, Nolan." Quinn had been writing a letter to Myra, waiting for his shift at picket. There was far too much grumbling in camp lately.

"Just watching the sun set on our final resting place."

"That kind of talk is bad luck," Kendrick crossed himself.

"No, My Friend, bad luck was drawing the short straw that put that joker up there in command of good men. I am going to kill that Son of a..."

There was a flash of careening stars, then black. Nolan lifted himself out of the mud. Had there been a solar collision or had he been shot? Quinn stood over him flexing a blistered fist.

"What in the hell is going on here?"

The clipped Irish brogue...it could be none other, "Evening, General." Kendrick snapped a half-salute.

Meagher stepped out of the fog. "Ah, Mr. Giles. Yes I remember. Every time I see you, Corporal, you are carpeting the ground. And Mr. Quinn. Two of General Kimball's more soft-spoken, parsons."

General Meagher regarded the little tarrier with a twinkle. The General liked his evening walks, away from the bustle of aides, orderlies, and papers. A cigar and a few minutes alone helped settle his mind. He liked to be among his men. And he knew that Quinn might be down here.

"General." Quinn's saluted then he leaned down to pull his friend to his feet. In the past few months, he and Meagher had met discreetly to talk of the old fight, of Quinn's father and Meagher's offer of a staff position. The General had taken on some of the image of the father he barely knew, and if there had not been a Fourth Ohio Quinn would have taken him up on it.

Nolan breathed in the heavenly smoke of the General's cigar — sweet even if it were fouled with the sulphur of the artillery exhaust. The General smiled and reached into his great coat for a silver case, "Gentlemen, would you please? Consider it an early Christmas present."

The four imbibed. Kendrick pulled a match and lit the ends of each of the three virgin cigars and then his own. "Private, mine seems to have gone out." General Meagher leaned into the flame that burned into the private's fingers. Kendrick concentrated on keeping his hand steady while the General pumped on the end of his cigar exhaling like a camel-back locomotive. It would not due to set the General's mustache afire.

"Thank you, Private."

"Welcome, Sir." Kendrick drew on his own cigar and found himself reeling. Nonchalance was not going to be easy as this was his first cigar. He had promised his Baptist mother he would not smoke, curse, or carouse. He would faithfully attend services, write her weekly, and read his Bible. Now his last vow was literally going up in smoke. God, who was the best friend of all righteous mothers, wasn't losing a second in making him pay for it. He nursed the cigar as long as he could before taking another puff. He did not want to insult the General, but he was feeling puny.

Kendrick drew on it and struggled to keep the smoke

out of his windpipe. His stomach heaved and rolled over. "Jesus, Mary and Joseph, don't let me be sick all over the General's shiny boots."

Thankfully, Meagher was moving off. "Good evening, Gentlemen. And Mr. Giles, be careful. We wouldn't want you to be breaking your leg before the battle."

"Yes, Sir."

The three pickets went on puffing exuberantly. "Smoking on duty, Gentlemen?"

For a big man, Sergeant Chase was remarkably light on his feet. "It's all right, Sergeant, They were a gift from General Meagher." Kendrick offered the Sergeant his cigar and backed away for some fresh air.

"Is that a fact? And what great heroics have you been up to that Generals would be treating you four hoodlums to cigars?" Chase bit off the end, slipped the stub between his teeth, and inhaled. "A good brand. You must have traded a whole wagon load of your naphtha for these. Mr. Kendrick, God bless you for sharing your good fortune with your Sergeant. God will be rewarding you. You're looking kind of peeked, Lad. You all right?"

Kendrick's cheeks bulged and he swallowed hard. "Excuse me, Sergeant. Permission to leave my post!" Without waiting for a reply, the private let off into the woods.

"Make short work of those stogies. The Lieutenant might have less patience with your fiction then your kind-hearted Sergeant." Chase looked at his cigar and nodded at its quality, "Good evening, Gentlemen."

11 December 1862
C Company, 4th-OVI
II Corps Army of the Potomac
Falmouth

Myra,

How I remember the gift you gave me our last Christmas together. The black eye for stealing a kiss right under the hay shute where your father was working. Sometimes a man doesn't see a black eye as a blessing of fortune until he realizes it could have been a butt full of shot. I carried that gift to dinner. Nolan made great sport of it, "Been singing Ave Marias around the horses again."

These memories come like embraces tonight as we ready for battle. They are as soothing as prayer and as warm as a camp fire. You see, Myra, I fear that is all we will have of each other.

Tomorrow we march into Fredericksburg. The enemy is entrenched up on the heights with all his might — and — well the Army is going to have a hard time pulling him down. I do not feel that I will live to see how it comes out. It is not fear nor cold dread that haunts me, but a knowledge and a relief — do not think me a coward — that peace will come sooner for me than the others.

I tell you this now because when you find me dead, you will not expose our secret by shows of grief. There is no longer any reason for your father to know about us.

I don't know what lies beyond, or what form heaven or hell takes because I deserve some of both. But if there is anything to faith in a divine reward, God will give me a chance to see you again. And when you think back on our time together do so with a smile and not tears. I wish to be carried lightly on your shoulders not heavy in your heart.

You must live well the peace that we fought for. This war will extinguish itself one day. If men have learned anything at all from this, they will have learned the cost of hate and the blessings of patience.

Don't think me a coward or fevered, I sleep in the comfort that I did the best I could. I could not have come to admit this without Nolan. I admire him. He wears his courage lightly, I have leaned upon it more than he knows. He is a man with promise, but I am troubled for him. If he should survive this war he will come home to no one except my mother. Among the 4th he has strong friends. But the unthinkable injustice would be for war to have blessed him more than peace.

Already this war has gone on too long. We have rounded the bend from the sons and fathers dispatched with parades and flags to become the cursed war itself. When he comes home — and God would not be so cruel as to take both of us — befriend him and love him as I have.

Quinn

XXIX

When Hunt's cannons were pulled back, Fredericksburg was a ruin. Trees like the claws of black skeletons snapped charred branches into the wind. Buildings burned like caldrons spewing columns of steam and acrid smoke. Plumes shot up from warehouses and homes erupting like volcanoes and burning like torches into the night. Through jagged window panes velvet draperies billowed in the winds like banners. Streets were littered with wood, glass, brick and mortar. A section of chimney lay across William Street. Pages of sheet music skidded across the brick like dried leaves, a shattered bowl of a clay pipe stabbed the ground. The gardens were littered with slivers of mirror, pieces of silk and lace drifted on the bushes like tiny pennants. The elegant Hanover Street was pocked and rutted, shells having torn trenches through the brick paving. Intersections were choked with rubble.

At first light the Fourth formed at the head of the Brigade, Captain Mason ordered the men over the pontoon bridge. The leafless trees and bramble covering the river bank were empty now of sharpshooters and all resistance. But they rustled in the pre-dawn breezes, beckoning them on.

"Attention! File-Right! March!" Nolan and Quinn stepped off. "They ain't going to shoot." Nolan studied the deserted river bank. "They want us to cross, to suck us under their sights where they can get a good shot. Never interrupt an enemy when he's making a mistake. Was that Chase or was it Napoleon?" Nolan smiled, "Same difference." Nolan indulged in the fantasy of about facing and raising mutiny in the troops. If they would mutiny for McClellan, damn, they would burn Burnside at the stake for a can of milk.

Quinn had been as silent as stone while they formed

up. Christie had prattled on mindlessly about setting up a shop back in Delaware with the pay he had been sending his mother to save.

The column halted at the edge of the shattered town. A Confederate corpse frosted in snow sprawled behind the picket fence of a withered garden. A hatless head slept on the sill of a broken window. A boy, his feet in rags and a tattered home-spun jacket gathered over his chest huddled still in a doorway. He must have been wounded there then froze to death. The cold had preserved him in perfect repose.

Beyond a fire still burned in the first floor of a shop, the windows and doorway aglow like a jack-o-lantern. Kendrick moved on silently. Good man, Kendrick, Nolan thought. I wished I had said so. Christie chirped on. It was harmless thinking aloud. His cud was none of the usual sort that most of them chewed on — the generals, bad gun powder mixed with sand, bad tack crawling with worms, bad sauerkraut, and all. He prattled like the only man in the Army who saw a future that day.

The Brigade eased. The skirmishers studied the windows and dark voids. The town was empty. But the sensation of being watched, studied, measured was strong. Veteran fighters fidgeted no matter how hard the officers tried to keep them formed up. Christie stepped back and studied the surroundings. He did not like them. Nolan agreed. He felt suffocated after a year of fighting in the open. The buildings came right up to the streets to close the men together. Shifting his weapon on his shoulder, Christie backed toward the door and turned the handle. It was locked. General Kimball rode up and down the column, "Easy, Men! Remember who you are."

They were ordered to close ranks and close mouths. Captain Mason issued the instructions for the night and

212

dismissed the men to camp and rest. They would go up at dawn. Occasional shots echoed down the streets as tenderfeet shot at chandeliers that looked like sharpshooters, at curtains and mirror reflections...at ghosts. The rifle shots were electrified by the artillery haze and fog billowing down the streets. It all spooked the Army with a brain fever.

Mason bivouacked the 4th, 8th, and 1st Delaware along the river. More rifle shots. Shouts. The Army began to fray at the seams. At first just to find suitable shelter indoors for the first time, to be off the ground, to even find a bed. In spite of the sergeants the men drifted off.

A window crashed like a pistol shot. "Easy men!" Colonel Mason galloped off to see about orders for the morning. Some of the company inspected an abandoned church, others put gun butts to elegantly carved doors and broke through. Still others pulled up bricks from the walkways and tested them in their hands. A window exploded. Veterans cocked hammers.

Ranks melted away in small swarms. Then the Army was wavering, veterans and tenderfeet alike melting off. Sergeants and junior officers pulled men back to the ranks only for it to leak someplace else. Another window crashed. The dam broke.

Giles uncorked the reserve canteen. He took a long draw on the elixer to control the tremors in his hands. He passed it to Quinn. The great Southern city was at their mercy. His friend shook his head but Christie took and nearly emptied it. Demons floated around them. It was Friday the twelfth, not thirteenth, but the night was going insane. Nolan sweated under his great coat, the icy winds blew the sweat away to make him shiver all the more. Blood pounded through his temples. His body would not be still. He was awakening from a long spell of sleepwalking through the oblivion of a succession of Virginia battlefields, all anonymous now — all of them futile, with road signs, "This way to defeat!" Orders barked in his brain, "By right file into line! By file, fire!"

"General Patrick will be on 'em hard when he finds out." Quinn hissed of the hard-nosed Provost General whose troops would be tearing through the town shortly gathering up raiders. There was nothing subtle or stealthy. The Army had disintegrated into a mob, filtering down through the streets, breaking through the doors, funneling into the second stories. The army was drunk, men danced as if clowns in a carnival.

Two privates pulled a rosewood parlor piano into the streets. In a frenzy others filled it with river water and a teamster led the wagon mules up to drink. A mudsill stumbled down elegant steps taking care to protect the heirloom decanters of port tucked in his arms. His cronies relieved him of their contents, passed them around until the bottles were empty and the crystal smashed against trees.

A single Provost trooper rode up hard shouting for order, calling up the sergeants to get control of their command. Men swarmed around the horse and it reared. They pulled it down by the halter and tore the officer from the saddle. He was swallowed up by the mob, stripped, beaten senseless and heaved down the cellar steps.

A barrel-chested private in a filthy uniform waived the trooper's watch over his head like a charm. "We take no prisoners, Men. We'll have our little fun!" He punctuated his sentiments with a succession of shots from the provost's Colt. When it was empty he threw it down the well and it clattered against the window grates.

Nolan pushed through the rollicking soldiers to where the officer huddled. He bent the head forward and brushed away the black, blood-soaked hair. The breathing was shallow and irregular. At last he opened his eyes. They fluttered randomly but finally focused on the corporal. "They are crazy," he gasped. "Arrest them." His head collapsed onto his shoulder and he rolled over.

Nolan settled the man back and wiped the blood from his hands. He pulled Quinn away by the shoulder, "He'll have a good headache tomorrow but he'll be all right. If he has sense enough to pretend he's dead."

"Let's get out of here before we get trampled, arrested, or worse. If we aren't good they may lock us up." Quinn could find no way out. The streets were a flux, men zigzagged between houses to find some undiscovered treasure. Nothing was too small to escape their notice. Inside mirrors and glass exploded, heavy shoes tore at the carpeting. Scavengers pushed each other out of doors grasping some small souvenir and then fought who had the rights to it.

Giles was repelled by it. As a corporal he should have been restoring order, but he wanted to be away. To finally be alone, to draw some breath by himself for the first time in a year and a half. Events coursed about him. It was the sensation he had in the first battle, of being in the midst of it but not being part of it — of being immune to fire or that he was already dead. Quinn's warnings were snuffed out by the obscene chorus of a drinking song, and the explosion of an emptied decanter. Troopers in hooped petticoats, and shawls jigged and capered. Others clapped hands, another sawed through a violin with a bow until the strings burst. He smashed it against a wrought-iron fence and clapped his hands in time. The Army whirled like a cyclone spilling debris and havoc as it went.

Shots rang out an upper-story window. A man leaned out waving dueling pistols. Blood and madness made him grotesque.

Nolan cut away from Quinn's grasp. He pushed and shoved against the tide to draw a breath. The mob surged around him, buffeting him, ricocheting him off one another. A soldier toppled and whirled around with a fist in mid air, striking Nolan in the ear. Nolan skidded against the curb. Men kicked and tripped over him as they surged down the street.

A soldier, Nolan recognized as one of the Fourth ran by him, his arm full of watches. Nolan swayed as if fighting gale force winds. He staggered. Turned. And ran.

Quinn shouted for him, but Nolan was lost in the sea of great coats and forage caps. He pushed through the swarm of men. He wanted only to be by himself. To be alone before tomorrow.

The snow chilled the steam on his cheeks. Nolan moved away from the shouts, the hurrahs, into the gray darkness. He drifted through the troops crazed by despair. No one stopped him, questioned his direction or intent. Beyond the town where the river bends around the heights, beyond the pillage of the cannon, Nolan floated.

He did not know how long he had been running, when he suddenly stopped and went reeling through a white picket fence. It splintered and he collapsed into a garden. Beyond, nestled in a cluster of spiny trees, was a white clapboard cottage, whole and untouched by the cannonading. He drew to it keeping to the shadows, cautious for dogs.

Nolan stepped under a portico and turned the handles of the French doors. Nolan could find nothing beyond the beveled panes but darkness. He twisted the handle again. Locked. He raised the butt of the Enfield and smashed a plate through. The crack of the glass exploded in his ears. No one came. Nolan reached through the frame of ragged chards for

216

the latch, raised it, and pushed the door open.

He waited, the blackness beyond did not ripple with a candle or lantern. Nolan struck a match and stepped inside. He tore at a piece of curtain and touched the flame to it and let it fall. The flame burned slowly up toward his hands. Nolan touched the rag to three tapers and pulled the sconce from the wall. The room glowed. High-backed chairs danced in the shadows, and louvered glass of corner cupboards reflected back rows of candles. Nolan enjoyed the sweet fragrance of scented bees wax. The dining room was big for such a small house. The sheen of the table was a mirror. His foot caught in one of the empty picture frames that lay like hoops against the walls. In the glow of the candles wallpaper shimmered like moonlight on a pond. There was a genteel world under their fiery politics. Did gentlemen discuss slave prices at this table over lighted cigars and brandy? Did they curse Union men as cowards, to be killed for sport and toast the cause of all good Anglicans? Did ladies entice proposals from giddy gentlemen starry-eyed and lightheaded from too many compliments, port and cleavage?

"My father couldn't scrape enough between his pulpit and his stubby farm to buy one of these chairs let alone this house. Giles counted them — four on a side and one at each end. Kathleen could be a queen in such a place. Giles ran his fingers along the backs that rose from the seat like elegantly-carved lyres, the arms seemed too delicate to support a man comfortably.

He tried to conjure an image of the woman who ruled this domain. Was she young and arrogant or old and crepey, with stiff, blue-veined fingers? If she were here would she laugh or sneer at this unholy intruder? Mock his rough uniform, beard, his course speech? Nolan fancied her floating on a cloud of silk, skin like milk caressed in a bodice of lace, and tended by a platoon of slaves. Were the hands of this house's mistress kept white and smooth because of a black woman's labor? Would she sneer at Kathleen, her brogue, her calloused palms, and homespun dress?

Where was she? Did they just pick up and leave it all for another sanctuary further south? He had heard that Southerners had many houses — one for hot weather and one for cold. Was this the Cause?

Nolan shivered with rage. Keeping away from the windows the skirmisher moved methodically across the room to a white-paneled door. He took cover against the adjacent wall and pushed the door open, waiting. It drifted outward at the touch. No sound came.

Nolan moved on. A parlor with divans and high-backed chairs that glimmered with leaves and roses burnished in the silk. He had forgotten the name of such cloth. The room had been cleaned of anything small and valuable. Nolan glided to the windows and released the ties, the heavy drapes fell closed. He felt better.

The house was like a cage to a man who had lived outside so long. His chest heaved and his heart throbbed. There was not enough air and yet he hardly breathed.

On the other side of the center hall were two doors. The first already ajar. In the candlelight he chose the room that glowed with the soft pinks of ripe peaches. Wisps of silk hung from a canopy bed in billowing folds like a mist of white cobwebs and ruffles. He touched it and the cloth ran over his fingers like rain. He must hurry.

Giles tore through the room ripping open drawers searching through their treasures, rifling through books with gold imprint on rich leather covers. He settled into the work of finding something, anything, to take away with him. He must have some talisman of this Cause. He upended vases of dried flowers onto the floor. He kicked them out of the way, finding nothing, he dropped the vase on the rug. The porcelain crashed like thunder and vaporized. Nolan waited. No one came.

He moved more boldly through the room, running his fingers along carved panels, pushing against sides of the mantle for hidden doors to pop open. He pressed tense fingertips over the door frames for springs and latches, searched for secreted keys, and thumbing and poking carved furniture and moldings. Nothing.

Failure fueled anger. The armoire almost came down upon him as he ripped wide the doors. But Nolan kicked it back and pulled out the gowns, gloves, hats, brioches, shawls. Nothing!

A sweep of his hand across the vanity sent perfume carafes, painted miniatures and hair brushes crashing. He bent over for the miniature that miraculously survived. He held it to the candles. In tiny detail, but yet perfect was the profile of a girl on the edge of womanhood, her black hair parted in the middle and swept back in combs. Ribbons and ruffles caught roses of silk at her bare shoulders. The face was puckered like a rosebud, but the artist had not softened the black eyes to make them demure. They stared back cold and sharp. A woman of temperment...of little humor. He slipped the miniature into his breast pocket and moved on.

The canopied bed loomed like a stage. The bayonet tore through the silk shams with a hiss. He gored one pillow, examined its contents and then turned to another. Disappointed he ripped and slashed at everything until only tatters clung to his hand.

A doll huddled against the headboard, its porcelain face resembling the women in the miniature. He tossed it out of the way. Plaster, silk and gold sprayed across the floor.

Nolan froze. He lowered the candles to better examine the wreckage. The cheek and forehead was all that was left of the fractured face. But there was something secreted in the recess of the skull. He lifted it out. A string of green summer leaves, six of them as large as the buttons on his jacket, cascaded over his palm. Emeralds. He had seen them only once. The night he and Quinn had been posted sentry outside McClellan's Headquarters in Alexandria. The night of one of his socials. The ladies paraded past him in elegance their throats and arms bedecked with glistening stones. Such treasures, worn as if they were of no more value than pennies. He watched them pass, red, white, green stars, paying him no more importance than the lamp or the flags.

Kathleen deserves such a treasure. How he would get her to accept it he did not yet know, but she would. He slipped the necklace into his pocket with the miniature and turned to go.

Triumph combusted into alarm at the unmistakable crack of a hammer being drawn back. The skirmisher dropped to the floor as the report of a pistol nicked splinters from the polished mantel behind his ear. As he fell, the candles tumbled and broke free of their pods rolling in different directions behind him. Nolan had been so absorbed in his quest he had allowed himself to be ambushed. Now he lay pinned against the floor, in a narrow space between the bed and the wall. At his back a window seat set in a bay. But the octagonal window above was too high. He would have a bullet in his back before he could escape. He would not die that way. The Enfield lay against the French doors outside — a dreadful oversight.

"Who is there?" He shouted into the darkness. The door was ajar about eighteen inches and then void.

"Put the necklace back." growled the disembodied

voice.

"Show yourself! Are you one of us or them?" Was it Reb or another looter. It made no difference. The Army was insane, he could be killed by either with equal ease. He wanted to make the voice speak again to get a bearing on it, to figure out what it proposed to do — was it sane? "Show yourself, Friend!"

"I am not a Yank. You're the thief! Invader!" the growl rusted out into a spasm of coughs that tapered off into silence.

A horse galloped by. There was nothing yet to cause alarm on the outside. The broken panes would not be detected in the dark, and the rider would not come up unless there was a cause. The horse passed.

The back of Nolan's neck was hot. A trickle of flame grew bolder against the lacquered floors. It was inching up the folds of the sheers that hung from the windows in four long columns. The candle had caught on the puddle of fabric on the far side — too far for him to reach and put it out. It went up like paper. He stretched one foot beyond the cover of the bed. Another shot tunneled into floor only an inch from his instep.

The flames tracked along the fabric quickly. He did not have much time. It was already coming at his back across the carpet. Scorched wool made his eyes run. If he moved the gunman would pick him off before he even cleared the bed. Nolan spread his arms under the bedstead. A trundle bed added cover, but blocked that way.

Flames ate at the debris that skirted the rug and ignited the opposite curtain. It seemed like an eternity, his mind racing. There were two colums of fire at his back and a wave of smoldering flame licking across the carpet.

Nolan focused on the gunman. Two shots — if the

chamber were full, he might have four more. All he needed was one. A third shot shattered the oval mirror in the corner showering tiny knives over him, slivers tearing at his hands and the back of his head.

Southerners were born with guns in their hands. Shooting was more than sport, marksmanship was a matter of pride. A trapped Yankee was prey.

Acrid smoke swirled around the room in gray wisps. A cluster of feathers smoldered and exploded into flames. The carpet beneath him was slowly eating away toward him. He had to act quickly. Plans whirled like planets in his brain.

Back on the Peninsula he had been pinned by Rebel fire igniting a summer-scorched underbrush. The fire had spread like tinder and cut him off from his company. He had been terrified and disoriented. Quinn had crashed through the fence of flame to pull him to cover, Rebel shells cracking the brush setting more of it to flame.

Heat blistered against his back. There was no more time. If he did not move he would die. If he turned he would be shot before he could be out the window. The only way out was through the gunman.

Giles took inventory of his options. His hand brushed across his bayonet. A poor defensive weapon but not entirely useless. To offset the tedium of camp life he had played with it, throwing it at knots on pine trunks. It was a clumsy weapon, badly balanced, the men rarely used it in battle, better as candle holders or tent pegs. But he fingered it now with new respect. He shifted the blade onto the tips of his fingers testing its balance, finding its center.

Through stinging, watery eyes, he summoned every nerve to focus on the door, measuring off the probable range, taking in account for a small man. Aim low. He laughed, "Always aim low!" Chase's words of wisdom before every battle.

He fleshed out his target. Old maybe, crouched, bent. He pulled out a handful of cartridges, the powder and rounds firmly compressed within the rappers. He flung them into the flames and waited. The fire ignited the black powder, it hissed and flared, the lead popped.

Nolan rolled to his right extinguishing the flames that had begun to eat at his coat. Rounds flared and exploded behind him. The soldier sprung to his feet, pulled back on the blade and let it fly. He followed behind it.

Lead seared past his temple. A wail. Nolan plunged into the black void and carromed into a chair, bounding it against the wall. He fought for his footing again.

The steel had found its mark. The light from the burning bedroom illuminated the puzzle piece by piece. Someone huddled in the chair, in the last grips of death. Giles grabbed for the revolver, but the owner pulled it back. The chamber discharged and heat grazed his thigh.

Nolan wrenched the pistol from the hand, and slapped the body away. It heaved and lay silent. He turned the face to get a better look. A cascade of dark hair fell away from the face. The eyes shimmered like golden coins.

"Oh merciful God!" The woman was as light and fragile as a doll. He could have lifted her out of the wheelchair with one hand. The Yank had waged war on an invalid, a cadaver shrouded in silk only days from a grave. She choked and blood splattered on his face. Nolan extracted the bayonet from her shoulder and she wailed.

The Rebel had not fled with the evacuation, winter was a greater enemy than the invading Yankees. She had survived the shelling and would have probably survived the battle as well. Nolan shifted her into his arms to carry her out of the burning fire.

The eyes flickered and narrowed on him memorizing his face for an eternity. He had been right about their arrogance. In a heartbeat she clawed and tore at his eyes.

"I hate you all," she hissed. He slammed her back in the chair. She spat in his face. Heat beat against his back, the smoke was swirling around them. Then, he simply ran.

The garden was bright as midday, the house was a rising torch against the blackness of the night. Someplace pistol reports rang, men shouted orders. The riot was flickering out, with time on their hands the provost would soon be up to the house to investigate. He must not be here. But which way back? Night surrounded him on all sides.

The soldier spun trying to find his bearings. What way had he come? He groped through the shrubs searching for the drive, a road, a path to the river. Shock and disbelief burdened his exhausted body. He swayed and tumbled over the lose ground, turning for the direction he thought the garden to be. His ankle twisted in divots of thorns tearing around his shins. Pulling himself up again he tottered like a drunk, his arms pinwilling for something in the air to steady his balance — to point the right direction. He waited for the sounds of men.

A sleeve whipped away the grime and smoke from his eyes. He was sobbing. Nolan staggered into the darkness. For anywhere in the anonymous, cold darkness. Numb and disoriented, the veteran of the front line lost his presence — he was in enemy territory — he was vulnerable.

If he had some possession of his skills he would have prepared himself for ambush. Behind him a figure stole closer taking a measure of him, waiting until the madman was in the open. Nolan did not see him come on. The phantom moved in careful strides — ten at a time — slowly, waiting for the advantage. Just as Giles was about to fall again the figure

224

blindsided him, throwing the boy back, pinning his arms against his sides.

As if by reflex Nolan writhed and twisted against the attacker pulling him down. Arms tightened like a trap around Nolan's chest pushing the air up out of his rib cage. A hand stole across his face, pressing against his nose and mouth so that he could neither scream for help nor breathe.

Brogans dug and tore up the sod, Giles pitching and tossed the bear on his back battering and slamming its body against a tree. The arm held over his face, wool with the brass buttons of the Union Army glistened only an inch from his eyes.

A looter or a provost — death either way. His lungs exploded and he dropped to his knees. Surrender, slumping dizzily like a rag doll under the weight on his back. He was exhausted, accepting what came next — arrest, a shot through the temple. Or a silent, snap of the neck.

It was almost imperceptible but the grip eased only a fraction, enough to let his chest expand. Giles stifled the craving to pant to draw in the cold night air in gulps like water. But he let it drift into his lungs of its own accord, feeling crept back into his limbs. The fog lifted from his brain and it began to work — to plan.

Cold metal pierced his knee. The bayonet. His body still in a heap on the cold ground, he slid his hand under his coat to his belt. How could it be there? The blade was sticky and slippery with blood. His fingers traced passed the ring and caressed the cold blade and waited delirious with hope.

The burden heaved and panted like an animal. The grasp slackened and Nolan catapulted against his attacker. He pivoted on his left leg bringing his right knee into the soldier's groin collapsing the enemy in half. As it jackknifed Giles thrust the steel up into the breast and stepped back.

The attacker recoiled and collapsed. Life oozed in long, raspy groans, and the body quieted. Giles swayed precariously over the dead man, his own body heaving and choking. The house was an inferno, a pyre for the rebel woman inside. It exploded in a thunder clap and the roof crashed, a thousand comets rushing through the night. Nolan had survived two attacks. He had grieved for the woman, but not this traitor. He had killed many soldiers, and tonight the color of this uniform made no difference — he was enemy.

His legs numb, immovable stumps Giles weaved back and forth hypnotized by the fire light streaking like ribbons across the dead man's face. The skin glowed like a lamp, wisps of blond hair tugged from under the cap covering the face. A tiny sliver of white snaked down the jawline.

Giles rubbed his sleeve across his face again. His chest billowed, raising the piercing wail of an animal that has been wounded. He slapped the forage cap away from the deadman's eyes.

"No! No!" he prayed. Giles collapsed over the body, pulling it up from the frozen ground. The head fell back limp. Nolan wiped the blonde silk away, "Why did you have to come after me? Always trying to save me! Not this time!" Nolan stroked the damp blonde forelocks frosted with cold sweat. Brian Quinn did not answer.

Nolan embraced him, reached for the hand and rubbed at the stiffening chill. "God forgive me. Quinn, can you ever forgive me?"

It was the eyes frozen in the grip of death — an irretrievable mistake that could not be called back. Nolan was captive to it for the rest of his life. Nolan held his friend and rocked him back and forth trying to keep the body warm with his own heat.

A thunder of hooves and the call of men to draw

226

pistols and surround the house. Nolan closed the deadman's eyes, gathered the body up over his shoulder and made off into the night.

XXX

As the Long Roll called the men to the line Giles straightened his greatcoat on his shoulders. Sick and trembling, he mustered to his place in the ranks. Christie and Kendrick turned to him but he shook off their glances. He had given the barest account of his absence to the provost who had found him wandering near the riverbank. A hangover — probably found some of that spitfire the Southerns were so found of conjuring. No trace of Quinn. Nolan only mumbled that Quinn was with his own.

Christie took it to mean that Quinn had finally gone over to the Irish and was probably down with Meagher pulling sprigs of green from the Boxwood and nestling it into their caps.

Nolan had laid the body to the right of the Union lines, so close to the Alabamians that he could hear them talking from the rifle pits beyond Telegraph Road. They were already full of themselves as if they had already won the great battle — counting casualties like a round of poker chips. Premature, but not unfounded, there would be a horrible slaughter here today. A corporal threw a deck of cards into the gutter his lips moved in prayer.

General Kimball leaned from his steed to give the last instructions to Colonel Mason, who commanded the advance. The Fourth formed along the railroad cut beside Princess Anne Street with the First Delaware behind. On the right flank, the Eighth waited between the houses on Caroline Street. The Fourth and the Eighth would lead the assault, Company C the advance skirmish line. All morning cannon bellowed over at Hamilton's Crossing. Mason checked his pocket watch. He turned to the men, "Cheer up, my hearties, cheer up! This is something we must all get used to.

Remember, this brigade has never been whipped — don't let it get whipped today."

Back aways, General Hancock was shaking loose his Second Division. Profanity that would cowar a demon, sent up cheers and huzzah from his command. Meagher's Irish began to sing. The roll of the drums, the bark of orders, and they dressed their lines around the colors. A second shell tore at the upper story of the house beside them. The ground whipped and rolled as soon as they stepped off. Nolan grabbed Christie to keep from falling. Mason pulled his sword from the scabbard and pointed to the front, "Deploy skirmishers! By the left flank!" Kimball reigned up and shouted, "Move out now, Colonel, God bless you — good bye." Kimball charged off to see to the rest of his command.

Nolan, Christie and Kendrick moved to the point, Sergeant Chase behind. They would come up on the enemy first, clearing the road of sharpshooters and pointing the way. If there was a God, Nolan shouldered the Enfield that had been found for him, he would let him live only long enough to kill enough to make accounts even. The Eighth marched up Hanover Street, the Fourth parallel along the railroad cut. Converging canister fire blistered the lines as they drew up to the drainage ditch that transversed the meadow. The bridge had been splintered and all that guided the column across were the right and left runners. Under blistering fire the veterans crossed them as coolly as tightrope walkers.

Advance Rebel fire flashed from behind the stone fences, the hollows of farm houses and furrows of gardens. The ground tilted toward the Telegraph Road. "Forward on the double quick!" Nolan charged as a shell burst at his side. Kendrick dropped behind.

The Confederate skirmishers dropped back from behind their advance position. They dropped back across the plain to the stone wall that bordered Telegraph Road.

The blue troops came on, wave upon wave of them, and Fredericksburg evaporated to the rear. Mason, the blade of his sword flashing like lightning in the morning sun, ordered his men to close up and advance with all speed forward. Shell fire exploded holes in the line, as men crumbled others ran up and mended the seam. Nolan pointed to the wall only a thin line of stone at the base of the Heights. "There! Rush 'em back to hell!" The remnants of the Fourth, hardly little more than company strength now, closed around him.

General Hunt ignored his own order of one round every three minutes. Shells screamed overhead like a flock of birds crashing into the heights.

At first it was a thunderous roar, but then the ear is a queer organ. It can make sense of pandemonium, filter it down to the fine points the crack of muskets, the shouts of orders, the cries of pain, of bugles, of curses, of prayers, of screams. And as the mind eased on it, the groans and gasps of comrades as they fell.

Shells channeled through the ground, throwing dirt into Nolan's face. As the line came up within range the enemy fired case shot, and canister exploded hot rain over their heads. It tore away limbs, and drove men down as if it were a dead weight. Nolan lay on the ground. Chase had closed up to his left. Nolan rolled over on his back to reload. He tore at a cartridge, spit out the paper and rammed down the charge. When Nolan rolled back on his stomach ready to fire, Chase was gone. On the left Christie was keeping up a steady stream of profanity, by now he had cursed each Rebel back four generations.

Nolan reached for another handful of percussion caps and cupped them back in his palm. He was loading and muttering joining in the chorus of obscenities that rose from every man. His mouth and teeth were black with powder. His heart ached to pray, it would have eased him a lot. But he couldn't think how to start or would God even listen.

The hill had slivered open in a flash of white-hot fire. The Rebs must be firing in rows and Nolan's own shot disappeared into the vast open nothingness of sulphur smoke and noise.

Blood dripped from his nose and ears from the concussion of the cannon. His gun vibrated as he drew aim, the heat of the barrel searing into the wooden stock. It misfired. Nolan threw it down and reached for another and pulled the trigger. The sweat poured from under his cap and froze to his mustache and beard. He balanced on his left arm, loaded and rammed with the right. How long had he been lying on the ground, the rest of the Fourth crouched around him. He had not remembered the order, but there in the drifting smoke and dirt where they lay into the frozen earth, men of the Delaware came up beside but no further. The Rebel fire was too fierce.

The roar of the battle rolled over in his ears like a crash of a wave. The sun burnt out in the black smoke. Nolan rolled clear so as not to be trampled by the advancing Irish as they surged over him with the cry of banshees. Somewhere in the swirling darkness and the snapping of flags were the echoes of Hancock as profane as ever. Oblivious to the fire bursting around him, he shouted to his men to gather behind the New Yorkers.

XXXI

The precautions against dying "Unknown" were for nothing. When the Union dead and wounded were gathered up two days later many were naked — stripped by the shivering Confederates. Nolan was found under the remains of Sergeant Chase and a drift of other bodies. The Irish had rolled the wounded and dead into something of a wall as a means of cover. An ambulance driver had hacked Nolan out of the ice with an ax. The cold had thickened his blood to a trickle and the shell that seared off his leg had cauterized enough of the vein to keep him from bleeding to death.

Like the rest, his coat and shoes had been scavenged by the Rebels. Lying on the floor of the Lacy Library, blood from another man oozed under his neck. He was only dimly aware of the nurses and surgical cadets working to save his life. Nolan thrashed in an agony of pain and nightmares as a white gauze cone descended over his nose and mouth and chloroform dripped onto the peak. A doctor reached for a scalpel.

Nurses had been forced to tie his wrists to his cot to keep him from pulling at his ligatures. Nolan refused all efforts at feeding and spit out the water and brandy forced down his throat. Overhead a big man with long white whiskers grasped him in his massive arms and upended warm port down his throat. Nolan choked and gagged. Then soup rushed past his throat, and he was helpless to resist. Nolan fought life, but it would not let go of him.

Giles awoke to see Christie hovering over him with an ungainly smile stretched unnaturally across his face. "Well Lad, you're going home with the biggest portion of the body you enlisted with. You was lucky — real lucky.

"Didn't you hear us calling you to fall back? Like you

was going to charge Bobby Lee yourself or die trying. You will make out all right if you don't plan on being no ballet dancer." Then his eyes turned sad. The comrade checked who might be listening and bent down, completely shutting Nolan in darkness as he whispered. But soft tones don't come easily to a man whose job it is to be heard above the battle roar.

"Your Pard won't be joinin' you, Nolan. He's dead. Naw, rest easy... don't be fussin' it's the sad truth. We ain't sure how he died, but he wasn't on the line. He was up on the right. Probably bushwhacked on one of his famous walks. Not shot neither. They must have pounced on him, tore his heart out, then stripped him.

"Look, I'm sorry, I needn't have said all that. But he died quick. You can be comforted by that.

"I wish there was some better way of telling you all this. You were screamin' for him in your sleep. As bad as it was. They came to get me...well, you had a right to know. The Captain will be writing his mother, I made him promise.

"Not much of the regiment left — the Irish are even sparser. Now you rest easy. Take this." From the sling that held his battered arm, Christie pulled an amber bottle and slipped it into Nolan's blankets. Then he was gone forever.

Throughout the long months in the Alexandria Hospital, Giles grew stronger. Death would not rescue him of his guilt. It was there the nightmares and sweats began as a regular part of his torment.

The news of Fredericksburg soared like vultures on the wind. Newspapers savaged the Lincoln who had raised up still another blunderer. Accounts deplored the defeat, of wave upon wave of men who refused to be labeled cowards slaughtered before that stone wall. Burnside was vilified as a coward, a butcher, and a fool.

Preachers thundered from the pulpits that an army of looters, wanton and unheeding of God's Divine Law against stealing was dealt with righteous fire and brimstone. In the shops and at the firesides of the Union, the faithful began to whisper that perhaps the war had gone too far.

Captain Mason had listed Quinn along with the rest of the battle dead. Rumors from the front drifted back to families in Dublin and Delaware that maybe the son of the Irish rebel was a coward and a shirker. Veterans believed otherwise. Quinn was a hero, killed scouting the lines, perhaps by a picket.

Nolan quelled the rumors with letters to the editors of the *Standard*, *Gazette* and the *Ohio State Journal* that Quinn had died surveying the lines — risking his life for the intelligence that would save his friends. He charged naysayers with treason — or worse cowardice for disparaging such a hero.

No one ever called her boy a shirker to her face, but whispers hushed as Kathleen entered the dry goods store or the post office. Faces turned away as she hurried along the walk to obtain a wagon and team to retrieve Nolan from the train station in Columbus. She had finally made him see that convalescence at the farm was only right. He had protested but she would not have him cared for by strangers.

XXXII

With one of Quinn's brothers at each elbow Nolan half walked was half carried into the little church. He had refused every invitation of a medal until Kathleen made him see that it was the town's way of doing him honor. She had urged him to go. But if he went she must go with him.

The Catholic sat openly in the front pew, sang English hymns and prayed from the Common Book of Prayer. When the time came, the rector motioned the veteran to the pulpit. The twins eased Nolan down the aisle and the congregation shifted nervously in their seats. At the front, he stood numb and furious as the rector pinned a medal to the blue jacket of his uniform. It was still his only suit of clothes.

It flickered in the morning sun like a golden new copper, suspended from a tri-color ribbon. Nolan pulled it from his chest and looked down on it resting in his palm.

The faces that two years ago would not have given him a second notice lavished pride on him. He hated them, but more than them, he hated himself. He was the biggest liar of them all. He wobbled on his crutches and the boys steadied him. The congregation waited. Nolan knew he must say something. What of the truth could he give them?

"I wonder what Quinn would say here, or Sam Johns, or Jamie MacGowan. But I cannot second guess the dead." He began slowly, staring into the faces before him one at a time. Memorizing them all. "The dead have the last word and they choose to keep it from me. But actions speak as a narrative of what a man is made of. The soul of an Irishman, or a Scot beats with the drum of freedom. He will tolerate nothing less than liberty, longs for it, prays for it, fights for it down to the last breath. It is the wellspring of his honor.

"Brian Quinn honored his father — and his mother —

235

his Church, the country that bore him and the country that adopted him — every day of his life. He performed the least of his duties so well it was noble, and the greatest and last so well it was menial. Taking the daring step to the head of the line was as casual as breathing.

"A skirmisher is the first to die, the enemy shot that cuts him down is his sacrifice...his warning to his pards — his comrades — to take the action that will save the most.

"I am here because Quinn is not. Because you do not meet here to honor him, I am not honored. Until he is honored — and his family — I will step to the back of the line.

"There is confusion as to what this war is about. Some say it's about freeing the slaves. Others say it's about holding tight the Union. I don't know about that. What I do know is what I hear on the battlefield after the cannon and guns have been pulled back. There's a fog that drifts over the men who lie there. And as it lifts and floats away, the men begin to call out. It ain't for Frederick Douglass or Abraham Lincoln they call for. It's a sweetheart... a wife... Mother... Dad.

"If they go on fighting, you must fight for them. They cannot fight alone."

Nolan stepped back, picked up Ian's hand and placed the medal in it. "Small currency...pitiful repayment."

Kathleen's beautiful face held him, and he vowed he would give her something of a son — the best left in him.

On the other side, Myra Capwell sat at her father's shoulder. The tears fell unrestrained down her cheeks. The old farmer beamed at him. Nolan stared back dumbfounded: But of course...the correspondence from the war...he thinks we are lovers.

XXXIII

On 5 May 1864, the day Grant met Lee in the Wilderness, Giles married Myra. As the stroke of a pen ended four years of fighting at Appomattox Court House on 9 April 1865, their only child Quinn was born. In 1869 Grant placed one hand on the Bible and raised the other in oath of office and Giles had read enough law to pass the bar and do it honor.

But the war still raged within him. The days of work, success, and esteem, dimmed into nights of broken sleep and odious nightmares. Myra's love could not extinguish them. They flared up almost as soon as he was asleep and the theme was always the same. Nolan felt the heat as he drifted off to sleep. Then there was the fire. It grew until flames that encircled and trapped him. They licked his face and bore down on him. He could not breathe. Just as he would suffocate, there was Quinn floating over them like a cloud. Fingers of flames swirling behind them like the regimental colors. He stood in the center, beatific in his blue great coat and forage cap. The off-center smile and the scar, an outstretched hand as if to reassure mortals they had nothing to fear from the inferno. Quinn bid him come. The dream exploded and Nolan was screaming as he did the night in the Fredericksburg garden.

Like breasting the surface of some pond, Nolan broke into consciousness gasping for air, choking on the sleep as if it were drowning him.

Myra would be beside him trembling, afraid of him, helpless. Nolan turned from her, ashamed as if caught seducing another man's wife. She was so beautiful and he hungered for her touch, her soothing words, the caress of her face against his cheek. She would reach for him after he had drifted off and pull him to her. He would sleep peacefully

237

now, his head against her breasts. She would guard him against the night.

If she could only been taught as to what tortured men. What to say to soothe their demons away. She could not distinguish the words, only screams. He missed Quinn and blamed himself for his death.

Other wives talked of nightmares, how their husbands slammed themselves to the floor when surprised by a flash of lightning or a crack of thunder. Strong men powerless as babies to fend off the battles that broke their sleep. They walked into rooms of dark memories that flared anew with blazing cannon, of ragged flags, of friends extinguished in a cannon blast, of a furious route from which they screamed to be rescued. The wives had no advice to give her.

When morning came husband and wife met at the table as if nothing had happened. Nolan never drew consolation from other veterans, attended the regimental reunions, took part in the monument dedications or the preparation of unit histories. Nolan never spoke of his service or of Fredericksburg to anyone.

And she came to accept it. He did his best to cheat the nights of their punishing torment by filling them with work and responsibilities. Instead of rest when he was tired, he stoke the fire until it blasted into the little office. He worked until it burned down and his pen froze in his fingers. Then he would stoke the fire up again. Alternating the two extremes kept him alert until he dropped into his chair exhausted and slept. And the dreams returned. A man driven to such relentless lengths becomes a success in spite of himself. Nolan's law practice thrived. He did the work of three men. The local party ran him for state senator, and he served twenty years with such distinction and honor that there was even talk of governor. But he refused. He was burning out.

Nolan had no other life than his work and he became his work. It left him no time to be a husband or father, for family to entice him into intimate circles to become at home with what should not be his.

He did not look for the joy a man takes in a beautiful wife, a bright son, the friendships and camaraderie that success brings. He and Myra grew apart. After she miscarried their second child she moved to another bed. She would hurt no more. Her grief was nothing compared to his. Through the brick and plaster walls her husband's sobs and pleadings tortured her. But in the morning he was in control again.

Quinn, their only child did not understand such adult arrangements. He was confused and pained by the love and warmth his mother gave so easily and his father who gave none at all. Only once did Nolan embrace his son. The child barely ten and too bold for his age, slipped off a dead tree and into the river. Nolan cried out his name as the boy's head slipped down into the eddy and disappeared. Wild with terror the father dove down through the murky dark water, blind, feeling past the debris and weeds until the tail of his son's coat drifted into his grasp. A miracle. He heaved the limp body to the surface and pulled him to shore. The boy choked and sputtered. Nolan shouted his name until his son opened his eyes. When he knew he was safe the child leaned against his father's chest and sobbed. The father pressed his son to his chest and sobbed too. Quinn lay all night in his father's arms. On the morning, he awoke and his father was gone.

The breech was intractable. The day Quinn left to study at the infant university at Ohio State, he extended his hand for his father to shake. There was an instant, a flicker in the eyes, Quinn thought his father would embrace him at last.

The flame died and the man only nodded. The boy dropped his hand, turned and climbed into the stage.

Columbus might as well have been India for the distance that separated the two spirits for the next five years. And then it was the world, as Quinn's work took him away for longer periods of time. When he visited it was when his father was away on business. His neighbors pumped the hand of the young engineer and slapped his shoulder. Quinn was the son every man could be proud of — successful, dutiful, and respected. Nolan was a blessed man.

The bells were quiet now. Occasionally a musket popped, but the night was tired. It would be soon dawn. The truth would have its day.

What would they all think of him? A fraud? Hypocrite? Murderer? A confession made you powerless. Kathleen, Myra, and Quinn — he loved them so. Would they be merciful and keep it a private scandal? Would his name be forbidden in their presence? Would Quinn refuse his inheritance? His name?

Nolan buried his head in his hand. Even if he could not express it, he loved them with a consuming devotion. The paper rested in his palm like a deadly revolver. If he hurled it into the flames he would be free.

Nolan raised the last of the whisky to finished it off. A toast, "To your son, Quinn, I raised him as I thought you would. I gave him your name and now I give him to you."

The liquor burned his throat like molten iron. His heart twisted. The glass slipped from his hand and disintegrated into a spray of crystal. Nolan was powerless to stop the battle in his chest. With the next jolt it exploded with a force that heaved him out of the chair. He choked for air. He tried to pull himself to his feet, but his body recoiled again as if he had been shot. Nolan dropped over the table and rolled into the andirons. The amber bottle skidded away.

Nolan no longer felt pain, he was pain. With the andirons no longer holding back the logs, they tumbled and rolled free. They would have set the carpet afire if his body had not held them against the fire brick.

He smelled the pungent fumes before he felt the fire. With his one good hand he beat at the flames that seared his coat.

"Forgive me, Quinn, for I knew not what I did."

Myra hammered at the door. And then there was the shouts of a man. It was his son, shouting for him. "Oh my God! How long had he been here? He sounds just like..."

"I smell fire!" Quinn heaved against the door. The oak bounced against the lynch and the next push sheered it off. The two burst into the room. His son kicked the log back and gathered his father up in his arms. They moved to the cool interior of the room. Quinn had always thought his father such a giant, but he was as light as a child.

Quinn eased the tortured soul into the divan and padded a wet handkerchief to the reddened face. The purple lips vibrated wordlessly.

"Father, you will be alright. Mother has gone to ring the bell. Help will come. We will get a doctor for you. Rest now."

Nolan shook his head. He reached for his son's hand, "N-No, it's too late. I just want to rest here, stay with me until it's over."

Nolan reached for his pocket watch and pressed it into his son's hand. "The truth is in here and in the letter. Where is the letter?"

"Don't talk. Rest" Quinn embraced him as if there had been no chasms between them.

With the office door open the sheet skidded toward the flames. The updraft pulled it closer with each draft. It lurched over the hot ashes and ignited in a flash. It was nearly gone when Myra stamped it out. In another second she would have been too late to save it. Only a sliver was left. Barely a couple of lines. She read them quickly and handed the paper to her son. "It's for you." She could not speak anymore.

"No!" the man gasped and reached for it. "Not yet! Not Yet!"

As the room slipped away in a blur of tears, his son focused on his father's letter. When Quinn had finished, he pressed the slip of paper into his father's palm. Tears in such a big man made Nolan fear the worst. Quinn read them aloud from memory:

My Dear Son,

How I love you. My most grievous sin is that I could not be a father to you...

The rest had burned away. Nolan drifted into darkness. All was the fury of wind blowing against his son's last prayer: "I love you too. That is all I need to know, Father, that you loved me."

About The Author

Jeane Heimberger Candido attended the University of Dayton where she earned a Bachelor and Master's Degree. Her career has been in marketing and advertising, free lance writing, and newspaper reporting. She has written for *Blue & Gray Magazine*. This is her first novel. She lives in Columbus, Ohio, with her husband of nearly twenty-one years and her two children Anne Marie and Robert.

Pride Publications
Post Office Box 148
Radnor Ohio 43066-0148

<u>Show Your Pride!</u>

Pride Publications offers white 100% cotton tee-shirts featuring our muse logo in black and lavender, as well as full color Pride book cover tee-shirts featuring your favorite Pride cover, like the striking art of "The Redemption Of Nolan Giles".

And to celebrate the release of another Pride classic, we now offer Pride logo and book cover art coffee mugs! Sip your morning wake up call from one of our beautiful mugs while reading a Pride novel!

Tee-shirt: $15.00
Mug: $12.00

Send check or money order to Pride Publications
or call 1-800-910-1312.

Please specify size (sm, med, lg - xxx lg) and design desired.

Pride Publications
bringing light to the shadows
voice to the silence

Pride Publications
Post Office Box 148
Radnor Ohio 43066-0148

Pride Publications was founded by a circle of authors and artists in 1989. A publishing house dedicated to shedding light on misconceptions, challenging stereotypes, and speaking for those not spoken for. A press created for the authors, artists and readers, not just for profit. A company that is not afraid to march ahead, to bring words into print that are not only rich entertainment, but also new visions of our world. Pride's works are visionary, revolutionary twists from the norm. Over the years we have seen many changes but we have stayed true to our goals. We continue to embrace diversity and quality, to take on projects that others find "too wild, too risky, too truthful". At Pride we believe that risk and diversity are part of life. And life, in all its shapes, sizes, colors, beliefs and orientations should be celebrated! We believe in opening eyes.

For more information about Pride Publications,
or about how you can become a Pride Author,
Artist or Sales Partner, write to:
Pride Publications

Matters of Pride

Pride books are available from Inland, Bookpeople and direct.

Books and Plays

* designates limited first editions.
** designates forthcoming titles.

The Redemption of Corporal Nolan Giles. Fiction. Jeane Heimberger Candido. A rich, haunting tale set during the Civil War by a talented writer and Civil War enthusiast.

ISBN 1-886383-14-6 $11.95

***Annabel and I.* Fantasy. Chris Anne Wolfe. The tale of a love that transcends all time and all categories. Set in the 1980s as well as the 1890s....

ISBN 1-886383-17-0 $10.95

Bitter Thorns. Adult Fairytale. Chris Anne Wolfe. Magical, romantic retelling of Beauty and the Beast with two heroines. *From The Muse* fairytale series, #1.

ISBN 1-886383-12-X $10.95

talking drums. Poetry. Jan Bevilacqua. Lush prose-poetry plus. Love, life, empowerment. Exploring the strength and questions of gender roles in society.

ISBN 1-886383-13-8 $9.95

***The White Bones of Truth.* Science Fiction. Cris Newport. In a future where film stars are owned by the Studio and independence is illegal, revolution brews.

ISBN 1-886383-15-4 $10.95

***Fall Through the Sky.* Science Fiction. Jennifer DiMarco. Sequel to *Escape to the Wind*, Tyger and gang discover secrets and prepare to face the Patriarchy.

ISBN 1-886383-16-2 $10.95

Sarah's Dead. Fiction. Jennifer DiMarco. Five friends in Brooklyn lose a loved one to AIDS. Difficult but ultimately up-lifting. Not a safe story, an important one.

ISBN 1-886383-08-1 $8.95

Winter. Adult Fairytale. Jennifer DiMarco. A boy becomes the embodiment of winter and goes to find his season companions. Romance, humor, magic.

ISBN 1-886383-05-7 $8.95

Seasons of Fire. Poetry. Jennifer DiMarco. Award-winning collection. Cross-section of styles: dark, elemental, stream of consciousness.

ISBN 1-886383-07-3 $7.95

At The Edge. Play. Jennifer DiMarco. Haunting, humorous. Powerful, empowering. Two women find love and courage in the face of death.

ISBN 1-886383-11-1 $9.95

To order a Pride Publications title
send check or money order to:

Pride Publications
Post Office Box 148
Radnor, Ohio 43066-0148

Or call 1-800-910-1312.